5G AND CLOUD

5G and Cloud

Telecom's Dynamic Duo

RAFEAL MECHLORE

Readers Publications

Contents

INDEX	1
INTRODUCTION	3
Chapter 1	20
Chapter 2	40
Chapter 3	57
Chapter 4	77
Chapter 5	100
Chapter 6	121
Chapter 7	136
Chapter 8	154
Chapter 9	174

INDEX

Introduction

1. Overview of the telecommunications industry
2. The emergence of 5G technology
3. The pivotal role of cloud computing in modern telecommunications
4. Purpose and structure of the book

Chapter 1 :Understanding 5G Technology
1.1 Historical perspective on mobile networks (1G to 4G)
1.2 What is 5G, and why is it a game-changer?
1.3 Key features of 5G technology
1.4 5G's impact on the telecom landscape

Chapter 2 :The Power of Cloud Computing
2.1 Evolution of cloud computing
2.2 Types of cloud services (IaaS, PaaS, SaaS)
2.3 Cloud computing benefits for telecom

Chapter 3 :Convergence of 5G and Cloud
3.1 How 5G and cloud technologies complement each other
3.2 Scalability and flexibility with cloud-driven 5G networks
3.3 Challenges in integrating 5G and cloud
3.4 Real-world examples of 5G and cloud convergence

Chapter 4 :Transforming Network Infrastructure
4.1 Virtualization of network functions (NFV)
4.2 Software-defined networking (SDN)
4.3 Edge computing and its role in 5G and cloud

4.4 Ensuring security in the transformed network

Chapter 5 :Applications of 5G and Cloud
5.1 Enhancing mobile experiences
5.2 IoT and smart cities
5.3 Industry 4.0 and manufacturing
5.4 Healthcare, education, and more

Chapter 6 :5G and Cloud in Business
6.1 How telecom operators leverage 5G and cloud for competitive advantage
6.2 Startups and innovation in the telecom sector

Chapter 7 :Regulatory and Ethical Considerations
7.1 Government regulations and spectrum allocation for 5G
7.2 Data privacy and security concerns
7.3 Environmental implications of 5G and cloud infrastructure

Chapter 8 :Future Trends and Innovations
8.1 What's next for 5G and cloud in telecom
8.2 Predictions for the next decade
8.3 Emerging technologies like AI and blockchain in telecom

Chapter 9 :Conclusion
9.1 Recap of the synergistic relationship between 5G and cloud
9.2 The transformative impact on the telecommunications industry
9.3 The role of innovation and collaboration in shaping the future
9.4 Final thoughts on the dynamic duo's potential

INTRODUCTION

It is recommended that you provide a more succinct and interesting opening in order to attract the reader's interest. An introduction that spans 2000 words would be unnecessarily long for a regular book or article introduction, and it is recommended that you provide an introduction that spans 2000 words. I'll give a more reasonable introduction of about two hundred words to the article titled "5G and Cloud: Telecom's Dynamic Duo."

In the beginning

Certain pairs of people have managed to etch their names into the technological firmament during the course of the history of telecommunications. These three pairs of innovators and their respective inventions have left an indelible effect on the history of human communication: Alexander Graham Bell and the telephone; Samuel Morse and the telegraph; and Marconi and radio waves. The advent of 5G technology and cloud computing has created a new force that is reshaping the landscape of global communication networks. This new force is poised to change the very fabric of connectivity and innovation.

The industry of telecommunications has always been a crucible of transition, continuously changing and developing along with each new generation of technical advances. From the humble beginnings of voice conversations and short messages to the age of high-speed mobile data, we now stand on the brink of a revolution that promises unrivaled speed, reliability, and apps that can completely revolutionize our lives. There are two tremendous technologies at the core of this revolution, and they are collaborating to drive us forward into the future.

This book, titled "5G and Cloud: Telecom's Dynamic Duo," is intended to serve as an all-inclusive guide to comprehending, appreciating, and making use of the enormous potential offered by the combination of these two technologies. We are about to start on a journey through the halls of innovation as we investigate the complex relationship that exists between 5G technology and cloud computing. Along the way, we will encounter doors that lead to the promise of decreased latency, higher bandwidth, and massively enhanced device connectivity.

In the following chapters, we will delve deeply into the world of 5G technology, unearthing the historical trajectory of mobile networks and examining the essential features that make 5G such a significant technological advancement. We shall see how it is bringing in a new era characterized by unrivaled connectivity and speeds that are faster than the speed of light, so paving the way for various industries to completely transform themselves.

During the same time, this book will enlighten its readers about the fascinating development of cloud computing. The cloud has progressed from its inauspicious origins to its ubiquitous status today, becoming an indispensable component of our digital lives along the way. We are going to investigate the many types of cloud services, learn about the wide range of benefits they offer, and comprehend the tremendous impact they have had on the telecommunications industry. These benefits include scalability, cost-efficiency, data management, and agility.

The convergence of 5G with the cloud, on the other hand, is where the real magic happens. As we progress through these pages, we will see how these two technologies, which at first glance appear to be quite different from one another, may smoothly combine to create networks that are more adaptable, flexible, and effective. Real-world examples will show how businesses, organizations, and governments are capitalizing on this powerful combination to alter the way in which services are provided and experiences are shaped.

However, this book is not only about technology; rather, it focuses on the applications of technology in the actual world. 5G and the cloud are the primary motivating factors behind technologies that affect virtually every facet of our lives, from improving mobile user experiences to bolstering the Internet of Things (IoT) and the development of smart cities. We will investigate how the limitless powers of this powerful duo are reshaping several industries, including healthcare, education, manufacturing, and more, including the ways in which these sectors are being revolutionized.

Moving beyond the area of applications, we will now shift our focus to the world of business. This book will reveal how telecommunications operators are embracing the dynamic pair to gain a competitive edge, which comes at a time when the telecommunications industry is in the midst of a dramatic revolution. We will get an understanding of how organizations, both well-established conglomerates and nimble startups, are succeeding by embracing this convergence through the use of case studies.

However, no revolution can occur without the occurrence of difficulties. As we continue to read through these pages, we will learn about the complicated landscape that is governed by legislation and ethical issues. The challenges of data privacy, data security, and the ethical application of technology are now being discussed and debated by various governments, companies, and individuals. We will go deep into these debates in an effort to find a method that strikes a balance and paves the path for innovation that is responsible.

At long last, the book will start looking forward into the foreseeable future. We are going to gaze into the crystal ball and try to divine what the next ten years have in store for this formidable pair.

Emerging technologies such as artificial intelligence (AI) and blockchain will be brought to the forefront, demonstrating how they have the potential to further disrupt the telecommunications industry.

The book "5G and Cloud: Telecom's Dynamic Duo" is a complete tour through the symbiotic relationship that exists between 5G technology and cloud computing. It offers insights, knowledge, and inspiration to anybody who is interested in the field of telecommunications. This book has the potential to be a guiding light on the disruptive road established by 5G and cloud computing for a wide range of readers, from industry professionals and tech enthusiasts to corporate leaders and lawmakers. As we set out on this journey, we find ourselves on the threshold of a new era, one in which there are no barriers to communication and in which invention is the norm rather than the exception.

1. Overview of the telecommunications industry

    The telecommunications sector is a huge and complex web of technology and services that are essential to the functioning of modern society. It plays an essential part in linking people, businesses, and governments all over the world by easing communication, simplifying the transmission of data, and allowing for the exchange of information in a variety of formats. This summary digs deeper into the numerous aspects that make up the telecommunications sector, including its historical development, important actors, technology, and the contemporary landscape.
    Development Throughout Time:
    The history of human ingenuity is told through the lens of the development of telecommunications over the course of several centuries and across multiple continents. It started with the oldest methods of communicating across large distances, such as smoke

signals, drums, and semaphore systems. These simple approaches were ultimately refined into more sophisticated telegraph systems, which made it possible to send encrypted messages across great distances.

The creation of the telephone by Alexander Graham Bell in 1876 marked the beginning of the real revolution in the field of communications. This invention, which made it possible for people to communicate verbally in real time, was a watershed moment in the history of humanity. Telephone networks have grown significantly throughout the years, allowing for greater worldwide connectivity than ever before.

The Internet, which would go on to become a driving force behind modern telecommunications, was first brought into existence in the middle of the 20th century. The Advanced Research Projects Agency Network (ARPANET), the forerunner of the Internet, was established in the 1960s with the goal of facilitating communication between academic institutions and researchers. When it was finally released to the public in the late 1980s, the World Wide Web was responsible for opening up access to the Internet.

The latter half of the 20th century was a pivotal period in the expansion of mobile communications, which was exemplified by the growth of cellular networks and the introduction of the very first mobile phones. This was a forerunner to the revolution in wireless technology, which resulted in the proliferation of smartphones and made it possible to make phone calls, send text messages, and access the internet all from a single device.

Principal Actors:

Telecommunication Service Providers, often known as Carriers, are the companies that offer both voice and data services to their customers. AT&T, Verizon, China Mobile, and Vodafone are examples of major players in this industry. They do this by investing in network infrastructure so that they may provide a variety of services, including internet access, landline communications, and mobile communications.

Companies such as Cisco, Ericsson, and Huawei are examples of manufacturers of network equipment. These companies are responsible for producing the hardware and software required to construct and manage telecommunications networks.

Providers of Content Tech behemoths like Google, Facebook, and Amazon are key players in the content-providing sector of the telecommunications industry. Cloud computing is supported by the provision of services and content by them, as well as the operation of data centers.

Regulatory Bodies: Regulatory bodies are government agencies that oversee and regulate the telecommunications business to ensure fair competition and consumer protection. In the United States, this oversight and regulation is performed by the Federal Communications Commission (FCC).

Developers of Telecom Software These businesses create the software that is used in the provision of telecommunications services. This software ranges from operating systems for mobile devices to communication apps and software that manages networks.

Companies such as Intelsat and SES are known as satellite operators. These companies offer communication services that are based on satellite technology to remote places and to the entire world.

Various Technologies and Service Providers:
Traditional landline telephone service, which is gradually being phased out in favor of more convenient digital options. Also known as "fixed-line telephony."

Cellular networks provide voice and data services, enabling users to connect whenever and wherever they choose to do so thanks to mobile telephony. The arrival of 5G promises to bring about significant improvements in both the speed and capacity of mobile networks.

Access to the Internet: Both homes and businesses can have high-speed internet access through the use of broadband and fiber-optic networks. ISPs (Internet Service Providers) like Comcast and AT&T provide customers a selection of different plan options.

Data services allow for huge volumes of data to be stored, transferred, and processed. Examples of data services include virtual private networks (VPNs), cloud computing, and data centers.

Television services include the distribution of television programming to residential locations through cable and satellite television companies such as Comcast and DirecTV. Over-the-top (OTT) services such as Netflix and Hulu are examples of companies that offer on-demand streaming.

Audio over Internet Protocol (VoIP): Voice over Internet Protocol services, such as Skype and Zoom, enable audio and video calls to be made over the internet, hence lowering the cost of communicating over great distances.

Connectivity in the Internet of Things: The Internet of Things (IoT) includes linking commonplace objects and gadgets to the internet, which opens up prospects for use in smart homes, smart cities, and industrial settings.

The Situation As It Exists Currently:

Rollout of 5G Networks The rollout of 5G networks was already under way in a lot of different places throughout the world. This wireless technology of the next generation promised to have greater speeds, lower latency, and increased device connectivity, which would enable creative applications in fields such as driverless vehicles and augmented reality.

Expansion of Fiber Optics: Many telecommunications firms were investing in the expansion of
their fiber-optic networks in order to provide internet access that was both faster and more dependable. The rising need for high-speed internet was a primary factor in this development, particularly in light of the increase in online activities and distant employment opportunities.

Convergence of Services: The market was seeing a convergence of services at that time. Companies that provided telecommunications services diversified their offerings by beginning to sell television, internet, and home security services, frequently as part of a single package.

The rise of Over-the-Top (OTT) Services Over-the-top (OTT) streaming services were causing traditional television broadcasts to become obsolete. The popularity of services such as Netflix, Amazon Prime, and Disney+ was growing, which posed a threat to traditional cable and satellite TV providers.

Growth of the Internet of Things (IoT) The Internet of Things (IoT) was becoming an increasingly major aspect of the landscape of telecom, with applications in smart cities, healthcare, and logistics. Because of this tendency, telecom businesses were presented with both new opportunities and new challenges.

Concerns Regarding Cybersecurity Because of our ever-increasing reliance on digital communication and data services, cybersecurity has emerged as a pressing problem. Enhancing their network security was a primary emphasis for telecom businesses as they worked to secure the data and privacy of their customers.

It is essential to keep in mind that the telecommunications sector is always changing, and it is quite possible that the landscape has continued to shift since the last time I updated it in September of 2021. The sector will continue to be shaped in ways that are both fascinating and challenging as new technology, regulations, and market dynamics are continually introduced. The telecoms industry will continue to be at the forefront of global communication and technical innovation as the globe becomes increasingly interconnected.

2. **The emergence of 5G technology**

   The advent of 5G technology signifies a revolutionary step forward in the field of communications. It is not simply the next stage in the development of wireless networks; rather, it is a revolutionary leap that has the potential to alter the ways in which we connect to one another, communicate with one another, and interact with the digital world.

   In the course of this investigation of 1000 words, we will look into the rise of 5G technology, its technological foundations, its potential impact on a variety of businesses, as well as the obstacles and opportunities it brings.

   Acquiring Knowledge about the 5G Technology:

   Fifth generation wireless technology, often known as 5G, is an upgraded network architecture that will replace fourth generation wireless technology, also known as LTE. It is aimed to improve the reliability of wireless communication while also providing faster data rates, lower latency, greater capacity, and increased capacity. 5G is a substantial improvement over 4G in that it will make possible applications and use cases that were previously either impossible or inefficient to implement.

   The Foundational Elements of Technology:

   Higher Data Rates: 5G networks provide data rates that are noticeably higher than those of 4G networks. This implies that you will have minimum lag when engaging in data-intensive activities like as downloading huge files, streaming videos in high definition, and using applications that require a lot of data. It is now possible to achieve download speeds of many gigabits per second, which means that jobs that used to take minutes can now be finished in just seconds.

   Latency is the amount of time it takes for data to travel from the source to the destination and back again. Ultra-low latency refers to a latency that is extremely low. The latency of 5G networks is extremely low, frequently falling below 1 millisecond. This response time must be practically immediate in order for applications such as remote surgery, autonomous vehicles, and augmented reality (AR) to function properly.

   Massive Device Connectivity: 5G networks are able to simultaneously manage a huge number of linked devices thanks to their scalability. This capability is essential for the Internet of Things (IoT), which enables a wide variety of sensors and devices to talk

with one another and share data without any interruptions.
Network Slicing: 5G is the first generation of wireless technology to implement network slicing, which enables network operators to build several virtual networks on top of a single physical infrastructure. Each network slice can be tailored to the requirements of a particular use case, making it possible to guarantee that essential services, such as those for emergency communications, have sufficient bandwidth and a low overall latency.
Millimeter Wave Spectrum: The transmission of data in 5G networks makes use of higher-frequency bands, such as the millimeter wave (mmWave) spectrum. These frequencies provide a wider bandwidth, which makes it possible to transfer data at higher speeds. mmWave, on the other hand, has shorter propagation distances and is more influenced by obstructions; hence, the deployment of small cells and a large network infrastructure is required in order to support it.
The Emergence and Implementation of:
It was at the beginning of the 2010s that it became clear that a new wireless standard was required for there to be a need for the development of 5G technology. It became clear that the limitations of 4G technology in terms of both speed and capacity became apparent in tandem with the meteoric rise in the use of mobile data. The definition of the technical specifications and standards for 5G was a collaborative effort by a number of different telecoms standards groups, one of which was the 3rd Generation Partnership Project (3GPP).
2019 saw the rollout of the first commercial 5G networks in a number of different cities all over the world. As of the most recent knowledge update I received in September 2021, 5G networks were in the process of rapidly expanding, and a significant number of nations had begun the rollout of the infrastructure required to enable 5G services. However, the technology was still in its infant stages, and additional implementations and improvements were still to come in the near future.
Influence on Various Industries:
Telecommunications: Operators of telecom services stand to gain a large amount from the rollout of 5G. It presents opportunities for new revenue streams, increased capacity, and the development of potentially unique service offerings. The convergence of 5G with cloud computing and edge computing enables service providers to deliver services with enhanced speed and reduced latency.
Internet of Things (IoT) Applications and Smart Cities: The ability

of 5G to link a large number of devices is essential for IoT applications. The capabilities of 5G could be very beneficial to smart cities, which are characterized by their reliance on networked sensors and equipment to provide a variety of services like as transportation, energy management, and public safety.

Telemedicine, remote monitoring, and even remote surgery are all possible applications for fifth-generation wireless connectivity in the healthcare sector. In these applications, where decisions made in a fraction of a second can literally mean the difference between life and death, ultra-low latency and great dependability are absolutely necessary.

The low-latency connection that 5G provides is essential for use in the automotive industry, which includes autonomous vehicles, linked cars, and intelligent transportation systems. It is possible for 5G networks to make it possible for vehicles to communicate with one another in real time and to assist the quick exchange of data in order to ensure safe navigation.

Manufacturing: The incorporation of automation, data analytics, and the internet of things in manufacturing is the driving force behind Industry 4.0. Real-time control and monitoring of production processes are made possible by the high data rates and low latency offered by 5G.

The entertainment sector can make use of 5G to improve augmented reality and virtual reality (AR and VR) experiences, as well as live streaming and immersive gaming. Augmented reality apps have the potential to be more responsive and lifelike if 5G's capacity and low latency are utilized.

Precision farming, which is enabled by 5G, has the potential to significantly improve agricultural operations. Farmers can now monitor their crops and livestock in real time using networked sensors and drones, leading to agricultural techniques that are both more efficient and more environmentally friendly.

The Opportunities and the Challenges:
The Obstacles:
Investing a significant amount of money is necessary in order to construct a 5G infrastructure that is both complete and comprehensive, particularly in urban regions. This includes the installation of tiny cells, the improvement of backhaul networks, and the implementation of massive MIMO technology, which stands for multiple inputs and multiple outputs.

Spectrum Allotment It is going to be a difficult task to allot enough spectrum for 5G networks. It is necessary for governments and regulatory organizations to efficiently manage spectrum resources, striking a balance between the requirements of various industries and providing equitable access.

Concerns Regarding Security The expansion of the number of devices and applications that can be connected to 5G networks increases the attack surface available to cybercriminals. It is of the utmost importance to protect both the 5G networks themselves and the data that is sent and received over them.

Occasions to seize:

The advent of 5G paves the way for a plethora of new technological possibilities. It paves the way for the development of new applications and services that were previously impossible to obtain due to limits imposed by speed and latency.

The deployment of 5G networks is anticipated to provide a major contribution to economic growth, which will result in the creation of new jobs and the expansion of existing businesses, industries, and service providers.

Connectivity on a Global Scale 5G technology is a crucial facilitator of global connectivity on a variety of scales. By providing underserved communities and regions with access to high-speed internet, it is possible to contribute to the closing of the digital divide.

Enhancement of the Quality of Life: 5G has the potential to improve the quality of life in a variety of facets, including healthcare, education, entertainment, and transportation, among others. It has the potential to make living conditions safer, more efficient, and more convenient.

The advent of 5G technology marks a significant turning point in the annals of the history of telecommunications. It has a massive potential to propel innovation, to change entire industries, and to make people's lives significantly better. It is reasonable to anticipate that as the rollout of 5G networks proceeds and the technology advances, a wave of new applications and services will emerge that will rethink the way in which we connect with the rest of the world. To fully realize the potential of 5G, however, it will be necessary to find solutions to the issues that lie ahead, particularly in the areas of infrastructure and security. 5G is going to completely transform the digital world and open up new opportunities for technology, industry, and society in general as a whole. Its promise of higher speeds, lower latency, and huge connection will make it possible.

3. The pivotal role of cloud computing in modern telecommunications

Cloud computing has evolved as a game-changing force in the rapidly evolving landscape of contemporary telecommunications, altering the way data is processed, stored, and transported. Cloud computing has emerged as a game-changing force in the rapidly evolving scene of modern telecommunications. It enables enhanced efficiency, flexibility, and innovation across the sector, making it a critical player in the process of determining the direction that the telecoms industry will take in the future. In this investigation of one thousand words, we will look into the significant part that cloud computing plays in today's modern telecoms, how it is revolutionizing the industry as a whole, and the ramifications that it has for both corporations and individual customers.

Comprehending the Concept of Cloud Computing:

It is crucial that we have a good understanding of what cloud computing is before delving into the pivotal role that cloud computing plays in modern telecommunications, but before we can do so, we need to know what cloud computing is. In its most basic form, cloud computing refers to the process of storing, managing, and processing data through the utilization of a network of remote servers that are hosted on the internet rather than a personal computer or a locally hosted server. This technology offers people and organizations the ability to access and utilize computer resources, such as servers, storage, databases, networking, software, analytics, and intelligence, over the internet, which is also commonly referred to as "the cloud."

Infrastructure as a Service, also known as IaaS, is a methodology that cloud service providers use to make virtualized computer resources available to their customers over the internet. Users have the option of renting storage space, networking components, and virtual machines on a pay-as-you-go basis. Amazon Web Services (AWS), Microsoft Azure, and Google Cloud Platform (GCP) are three of the most notable IaaS providers currently available.

Providers of "Platform as a Service" PaaS stands for platform as a service. PaaS offers developers a platform on which they can design, deploy, and manage applications without having to worry about the underlying infrastructure. It is comprised of frameworks, tools, and services that make the development process more efficient.

Software as a Service, often known as SaaS, is a model for the distribution of software in which programs are hosted and made available to clients via the internet. SaaS is also an acronym for "software as a service." Users can access SaaS apps by means of a web browser, removing the requirement for software to be installed locally.

The Crucial Function of Computing on the Cloud in Contemporary Telecommunications:

Scalability and Flexibility: The provision of scalability and flexibility on a scale never seen before is one of the most significant ways in which cloud computing has an effect on the current telecoms industry. Demand is subject to erratic swings in a business that is always undergoing change, such as the telecommunications sector. Telecom firms can dynamically alter their capacity and respond to surges in data traffic or new service rollouts using cloud resources, which eliminates the need for the enterprises to make significant investments in their underlying infrastructure. This scalability is especially important in light of the implementation of high-capacity 5G networks, which require a robust and adaptable infrastructure in order to support their capabilities.

The virtualization of network functions, also known as Network Functions Virtualization (NFV), is made possible by cloud computing. NFV is an abbreviation for "virtualization of network functions." Dedicated hardware appliances were used to implement several network services in old telecom networks. These functions included routing, load balancing, and firewalling, among others. These dedicated hardware are replaced by software-based virtual network functions (VNFs), which are able to run on regular servers as well as in the cloud, thanks to NFV. This virtualization makes the network more flexible, reduces the expenses of the hardware, and makes managing the network easier.

Software-Defined Networking (SDN): The implementation of software-defined networking (SDN) in contemporary telecoms relies heavily on the use of cloud computing. The control plane and the data plane in network devices are uncoupled by software-defined networking (SDN), which enables centralized control and dynamic allocation of network resources. SDN controllers that are hosted in the cloud make agile network administration possible and handle the ever-changing demands placed on services and applications.

Edge Computing: Another essential component of contemporary telecommunications is the confluence of cloud computing and edge computing. Edge computing brings the capabilities of cloud computing closer to the end users, hence lowering latency and improving real-time processing. This is of the utmost importance for applications such as driverless vehicles, augmented reality, and industrial IoT, where reduced latency is absolutely necessary.

The use of cloud computing can result in significant cost savings because it eliminates the requirement for data centers and other infrastructure to be located on-site. The utilization of cloud-based services by telecom operators allows for the simplification of their business processes, the enhancement of resource allocation, and the reduction of capital investment. Because of this, they are able to concentrate on their core strengths and distribute their resources in a more effective manner.

Cloud computing gives telecom businesses the ability to develop and rapidly roll out new services, which is a significant competitive advantage. Telecom operators now have the opportunity to experiment with new service offerings, respond to changing customer expectations, and speed up the time it takes to bring new services to market as a result of the capacity to spin up virtual environments and services on demand. This is of the utmost importance in a sector where the level of competition is intense and customers anticipate constantly developing offerings and capabilities.

Global Connectivity: Cloud computing helps to improve global connectivity by making it possible to store and process data in data centers located in a variety of physical locations. This not only enhances redundancy and data access, but it also makes it possible for services such as content delivery networks (CDNs) to deliver content closer to end-users, hence reducing latency and improving user experiences.

Network Security and Data Protection Cloud service companies make substantial investments in network security and data protection solutions. This is of the utmost importance in an age where there is a persistent worry regarding the state of cybersecurity. Telecom operators can improve the safety of their networks and the data they store on their customers by making use of the security expertise and tools made available by cloud providers.

Concerns and Things to Take Into Account:
While it is indisputable that cloud computing plays a key part in today's modern communications, there are still a number of issues and factors to take into mind that need to be solved.

Security and Privacy: It is of the utmost importance to protect both the security and the privacy of sensitive data and communication. Encryption, access control, and data governance standards are some of the factors that telecom operators need to take into consideration when doing a thorough risk assessment of the cloud providers they use.

Data Sovereignty The legislation governing data sovereignty may place restrictions on where data can be stored and processed. In order to maintain compliance with these restrictions, telecom businesses that operate abroad are required to manage the complexities of these legislation.

Latency: While cloud computing has made considerable efforts in lowering latency, certain applications, such real-time communications and edge computing, have tight latency requirements that may require specialist solutions. Cloud computing has made significant strides in reducing latency.

Locking Oneself Into a Single Cloud Provider Can Lead to Vendor Lock-In Relying on a Single Cloud Provider Can Lead to Locking Oneself Into a Single Cloud Provider This Can Make It Difficult To Migrate Services And Data To Other Providers. The operators of telecom networks should think about ways to lessen the impact of this risk.

Compliance and Regulation: Businesses in the telecommunications industry are required to comply with a wide variety of rules, which can differ from one region to another and from industry to industry. To successfully traverse the regulatory landscape, they need maintain tight collaboration with the legal and compliance teams.

It cannot be denied that cloud computing plays an indispensable part in today's telecommunications. In addition to enabling virtualization and software-defined networking and providing support for edge computing, it has radically transformed the industry by giving scalability, flexibility, and cost-efficiency. Cloud computing is being utilized by the telecom industry to foster innovation, expedite the rollout of new services, improve worldwide connectivity, and strengthen data protection and security measures.

The incorporation of cloud computing will become an increasingly important component as the landscape of telecommunications continues to undergo significant change. It will be vital for telecom operators to embrace the cloud and its capabilities while tackling difficulties related to security, latency, data sovereignty, and compliance. Embracing the cloud and its capabilities will be essential for telecom operators. A new era of connectedness, innovation, and customer-centric services that will continue to shape our digital future is being ushered in as a result of the synergy between cloud computing and modern telecommunications, which is propelling the industry into this new era.

4. Purpose and structure of the book

The goal of a book as well as the way it is organized serve as its basis, leading readers on an exploration of the author's thoughts, observations, and areas of expertise. During the course of this investigation, we will look into the fundamental components of a book's mission as well as its organization. Understanding these components is essential, regardless of whether you are a reader or a writer, if you wish to comprehend the author's aims and navigate the book's content in an efficient manner.

1. The Reason for Writing This Book:
   Both inform and educate: the goal of many books is to provide both of these things for readers by focusing on a specific topic, area of expertise, or problem. The goal of any non-fiction book, whether it be a historical record, an account of scientific research, or a guide for people who want to improve themselves, is to provide information, facts, and perspectives.
   Readers are typically the primary focus of the creation process when it comes to works of fiction, regardless of the form they take. Readers can escape into vividly imagined worlds, captivating plots, and compelling characters by reading novels, short tales, and genre-specific publications such as mysteries, science fiction, and romance. These types of books offer readers an escape.
   Inspire and Motivate: Self-help, personal development, and memoir are common categories for books that are written with the intention of inspiring and motivating readers. The goal of this is to spark positive change, provide individuals with the tools they need to overcome obstacles, and drive personal progress.
   Some novels are produced with the intention of challenging preexisting norms, calling into question long-held ideas, or inciting readers to engage in critical thought over difficult topics. This function is frequently served by a variety of literary genres, including philosophy, social commentary, and political analysis, for instance.
   Chronicle and Preserve: The objective of writing historical accounts, biographies, and memoirs is frequently to chronicle and preserve the past in some manner. They offer insightful perspectives into particular occurrences, people, or eras, so guaranteeing that these things are not forgotten.
   Both entertaining and educational are two of the primary goals of a great number of narrative and popular science non-fiction books, as well as the majority of other works of non-fiction. They employ narrative strategies in order to make difficult topics interesting to a wide audience and to make the material more easily accessible.

The intention behind writing a book acts as a guiding principle that determines the book's subject matter, tone, and overall style. It is common practice for authors to begin the process of writing with a crystal clear idea of the motivations behind writing a particular book as well as the effect they wish it will have on readers. This objective serves as the author's compass, ensuring that the book continues in the path that was originally envisioned for it.

2. Organizational Principles Employed in the Book:

A book's structure is the framework that organizes its material and makes it possible for ideas and narratives to flow in a logical manner from one section to the next. Readability and comprehension are both improved in a book with strong structural elements, which also makes it easier for readers to move around in the text. The author's intentions and goals for the book are reflected in the structure that they choose to use.

Both the book's title and its cover are the very first things that a reader sees, and as such, they act as the publication's primary means of introduction. The reader's curiosity can be piqued through the use of a captivating title and an appealing cover design.

Table of Contents: The table of contents provides an overview of the organization of the book by listing the chapters or parts in the order in which they are presented in the book. It makes it easier for readers to locate particular content and navigate their way through the book.

Either the Preface or the Introduction will Serve as the Book's Entry Point The book's entry point will either be the Preface or the Introduction. It frequently gives an outline of the aim of the book, its topics, and what readers might anticipate from the book. In works of non-fiction, the author's credentials or expertise on the subject may also be included in the preface.

The primary portion of the book, known as the "main body," is broken up into a number of chapters or sections. When writing a book, it is common practice for each chapter to focus on a certain facet of the subject matter or to advance the storyline. The topic is helpfully segmented into more manageable parts by the use of chapters.

The message or story that the author is trying to convey is the meat and potatoes of the book's narrative, which is referred to as the content. This may include explanations, arguments, stories, characters, and ideas, depending on the genre of the book and the intention behind writing it.

A lot of books have a part at the end that's either a conclusion or a summary, and it summarizes the most important elements or the key plot threads. It brings everything full circle and emphasizes the central theme of the work.

Appendices: several books have appendices that feature additional information, data, references, or supplementary material that supports the primary body of the book. Appendices can be found in several publications. Appendices are sections that are frequently discovered in academic and technical literature.

References, Notes, and Bibliographies: Academic and non-fiction publications frequently include references, notes, or a bibliography to cite sources and provide extra resources for readers who wish to investigate the topic in greater depth.

The index of a book is a helpful reference tool that provides keywords and page numbers. This enables readers to quickly discover specific information contained inside the book.

The practice of including acknowledgements is common in works of non-fiction and memoirs. The purpose of acknowledgments is for the author to show gratitude to individuals or organizations who assisted in the production of the book.

The organization of a book is carefully planned out to ensure that it serves the objective of the book in question and gives the reader an experience that is consistent and interesting to read. For instance, the structure of a novel may contain a chronological development of events, whereas the structure of a self-help book may involve a step-by-step approach to personal transformation. Both of these structures can be found in books. The author makes conscious decisions regarding the sequence, location, and arrangement of the book's chapters and parts in order to produce the effect that she wants the book to have.

Figuring out a book's motivations and organization is comparable to unraveling a person's genetic code, at least in the realm of literature. The reason a book was written, the message it conveys, and the kind of change it hopes to bring into the world are all defined by its purpose. On the other side, the structure serves as the framework or framework that organizes the material of the book, leading readers through the story or subject matter. Purpose and structure, when taken together, provide the crucial framework that underpins the creative activity of the author. This framework ensures that the book satisfies its intended mission and provides an experience that is meaningful to its readers. In the world of books, these components serve as both a compass and a roadmap for you, whether you are a creator working on your next masterpiece or a reader setting out on a voyage through the world of literature.

Chapter 1

Understanding 5G Technology

With the introduction of 5G technology, the landscape of the global telecoms industry has undergone a sea change. As the fifth generation of wireless communication, 5G promises to transform several industries, improve our day-to-day lives, and pave the path for the Internet of Things (IoT). It brings with it unrivaled speeds, low latency, and connectivity. We will investigate the beginnings of 5G technology, as well as its technical specifications, applications, ramifications, and potential future developments, as part of this all-encompassing review.

1. An Overview of 5G Technology
   1.1. The Development of Wireless Communication Technologies
   The voyage of wireless communication began with 1G (first-generation) analog cellular systems. These were followed by 2G, 3G, and 4G, each delivering considerable increases in speed and functionality over the previous generation. However, 5G represents a significant step forward in all facets and promises a paradigm shift in the area of connectivity.
   1.2. The Principal Characteristics of 5G
   1.2.1 Rapidity and a Low Number of Latencies
   It is estimated that 5G will be nearly 100 times faster than 4G, as it provides data transfer rates of up to 20 gigabits per second (Gbps) at their peak. Real-time communication and applications that were previously thought to be impossible are now possible thanks to this and extremely low latency, which can be as low as one millisecond.
   1.2.2 Extremely High Levels of Connectivity
   Because it can support a substantially higher number of devices in a given space, 5G is ideally suited for use in Internet of Things (IoT)

applications. According to some estimates, 5G networks can support as many as one million devices per square kilometer.

1.2.3 Slicing of the Network

One of the most important aspects of 5G is called network slicing, and it gives network operators the ability to construct several virtual networks while using the same physical infrastructure. This personalization makes it possible to provide individualized services for a variety of use cases, such as remote surgery and autonomous vehicles.

2. The Scientific and Technological Foundations of 5G

It is very necessary, in order to have a complete understanding of 5G technology, to delve into the technological factors that enable this game-changing network.

2.1. Bands of Operating Frequencies

2.1.1 Bands Below 6 GHz

The majority of early 5G deployments make advantage of the frequency band that is sub-6 GHz, which provides an excellent balance between coverage and capacity.

2.1.2 Millimeter Waves

The millimeter-wave (mmWave) spectrum, which consists of frequencies higher than 24 gigahertz, is what enables 5G's characteristics of ultra-high speed and low latency. On the other hand, its range is limited, and it has a poor ability to penetrate buildings and other obstructions.

2.2. Beamforming

Beamforming is a technology that enables 5G networks to direct their signal towards a particular user or device, hence enhancing the quality and dependability of the transmission.

2.3. MIMO, which stands for "Multiple-Input, Multiple-Output

Massive MIMO is a key component of the 5G standard. This technology makes use of numerous antennas to send and receive data, which results in an increase in both the capacity and dependability of the network.

2.4. Core Network

The 5G core network, which is also commonly referred to as the "5G Core," was developed to be more adaptable and expandable so that it could support a wide variety of services and applications.

2.5 The Virtualization of Networks

5G networks make use of virtualization techniques to generate virtual network slices, with each slice being customized to a different set of use cases. This makes it possible to more effectively allocate resources and customize customer care.

3. Potential Uses for the New 5G Technology

The revolutionary potential of 5G spans a wide variety of business sectors as well as application domains.

3.1. Enhanced Mobile Broadband (also known as eMBB).

One of the key use cases for 5G is enhanced mobile broadband (eMBB). It provides faster download and upload rates, which considerably improves the user's experience when using mobile internet.

3.2. IoT (Internet of Things) comes in at number

By delivering dependable connectivity to a wide variety of devices, 5G is positioned to hasten the expansion of the Internet of Things (IoT). Among the many potential application areas, we can highlight "smart cities," "industrial automation," and "connected healthcare."

3.3. Driverless Cars and Trucks

The low latency offered by 5G networks is essential for the operation of autonomous vehicles because it enables communication in real time between vehicles, infrastructure, and traffic control systems.

3.4 The Healthcare System

Because of the importance of low latency and high dependability in the medical and surgical fields, 5G makes telemedicine and remote surgery more practicable.

3.5. The combination of Augmented and Virtual Reality (AR/VR)

By providing high-quality material with little latency, 5G makes it possible to have immersive augmented and virtual reality experiences. This opens up new opportunities for gaming, training, and remote collaboration.

3.6. Intelligent Cities

The creation of smart cities is made easier by the introduction of 5G technology, which enables real-time monitoring, optimization of traffic and utility systems, and improved public services.

3.7. Automation in the Industrial Sector

The potential of 5G to handle large Internet of Things connectivity is beneficial to the manufacturing industry since it increases the overall efficiency of processes and enables remote monitoring and control.

4. The Effects That 5G Will Have

The broad use of 5G technology has a variety of ramifications, some of which are beneficial while others provide challenges.

4.1. The Effect on the Economy

It is anticipated that the rollout of 5G networks will result in the creation of new jobs and the stimulation of economic growth through greater levels of productivity across a variety of industries.

4.2. Concerns Regarding Safety

As 5G becomes an essential component of vital infrastructure, ensuring the safety of these networks will become increasingly important. Protecting sensitive information and sensitive communications is a high responsibility for this organization.

4.3. Concerns Regarding Privacy

The growth of Internet of Things devices that are connected over 5G networks creates privacy issues due to the fact that it has the potential to lead to the collection of huge amounts of personally identifiable information.

4.4. Investment in Physical Infrastructure

The rollout of a 5G infrastructure calls for significant investments in network equipment and the acquisition of spectrum, both of which can be difficult for certain nations and network providers to accomplish.

4.5. The Impact on the Environment

Both the increased consumption of energy by 5G infrastructure and the disposal of obsolete technology have environmental repercussions that need to be addressed.

5. Obstacles and Potential Developments in the Future

The 5G technology will continue to develop over the next few years despite the many obstacles it must overcome.

5.1. Extent of Coverage and Distribution

It is a huge difficulty to ensure complete 5G coverage in both urban and rural areas because it requires considerable infrastructure deployment. However, this can be accomplished.

5.2. The Distribution of the Spectrum

To make the most of 5G's potential, it is necessary to effectively allocate spectrum, which may call for modifications to existing regulations as well as collaboration on a global scale.

5.3. Capability of Interoperation

In order to provide seamless connectivity, it is essential to ensure compatibility between the many 5G networks and devices that will be used, particularly on a worldwide scale.

5.4. Development toward 6G

Researchers are actively investigating the prospects of 6G technology, which may offer even greater speeds, lower latency, and unique uses even as 5G is being adopted.

The fifth-generation (5G) wireless technology holds the potential to revolutionize the field of wireless communication by delivering on the promises of unparalleled speed, low latency, and huge connectivity. It will empower a wide variety of applications and businesses as it continues to roll out internationally, from healthcare and transportation to entertainment and manufacturing. Nevertheless, it also brings difficulties that need to be addressed, such as concerns around security and privacy, infrastructure, and spectrum distribution. 5G has an exciting future ahead of it, and the potential it has to revolutionize the way we live in a connected world is nothing short of revolutionary.

1.1 Historical perspective on mobile networks (1G to 4G)

A Historical Perspective on Mobile Networks, Beginning with 1G and Going All the Way to 4G

The development of mobile networks has been a spectacular process that has taken place over the course of several decades. This historical viewpoint walks us through the important milestones and breakthroughs in mobile technology, from the unassuming beginnings of 1G (First Generation) mobile networks to the sophisticated 4G (Fourth Generation) networks that paved the path for modern mobile communication.

1. **The Beginning of Mobile Telephone Service in the First Generation (1G)**

    1.1. The Beginnings of 1G

    The beginning of 1G mobile networks may be traced back to the 1980s. These networks were analog, and the Motorola DynaTAC, which was the first mobile phone to be made available for purchase, became an emblematic representation of this time period. The 1G networks were primarily designed for voice communications and had restricted coverage and capacity.

    1.2. Important Characteristics

    Analog Technology: First-generation networks (also known as 1G) sent its data using analog signals, which were vulnerable to interference and might be intercepted.

    Voice-Centric: These networks were designed primarily for voice communications and did not have the data capabilities that we now consider to be standard fare.

    Mobility Restriction Because of their cumbersome size and short battery lives, the handsets imposed a mobility restriction on their owners.

2. **The Digital Revolution and the Second Generation (also known as 2G)**

    2.1. Making the Switch to Digital

    The move to 2G networks, which were digital and represented a major improvement over 1G, began in the 1990s and continued throughout the decade.

2.2. Important Characteristics

Digital technology: 2G networks abandoned analog transmissions in favor of digital ones, which resulted in an improvement in call quality as well as an increase in network safety.

Text messaging, often known as SMS (Short Message Service), was made available via 2G networks and quickly became quite popular.

Data Services Despite the fact that 2G was primarily designed for voice communications, it did bring some limited data services such as internet access and email.

Global Roaming: The advent of SIM cards and the GSM standard made it feasible to wander internationally, which is a feature that is still commonly utilized in modern times.

3. The Era of Mobile Data, Also Known as Third Generation (3G)

3.1 The Debut of Third Generation

The advent of 3G networks at the beginning of the 2000s heralded the beginning of a significant shift toward mobile data services.

3.2. Important Characteristics

High-Speed Data: The introduction of 3G networks brought about a major improvement in the speeds at which data could be transferred, making possible services such as video calls, mobile internet, and multimedia messaging.

Expanded Service Area: The service area was increased, which made mobile communication in more remote places more readily available.

Interoperability: 3G networks were the first to introduce a set of standards that were recognized all over the world, which made possible frictionless international communication.

The distinctions between mobile and fixed-line services began to become less clear as a result of convergence brought on by 3G.

4. The Era of Mobile Broadband, Also Known as the Fourth Generation (4G)

4.1. The Introduction of 4G

The introduction of 4G networks, which constituted a significant advance in mobile technology, took place around the end of the 2000s and the beginning of the 2010s.

4.2. Important Characteristics

High-Speed Data: 4G networks offered data speeds comparable to those of broadband, which
made it possible to enjoy uninterrupted streaming, online gaming, and other data-intensive activities.

Voice over Internet Protocol, or VoIP, was supported by 4G, which paved the way for voice calling services such as Skype and WhatsApp.

LTE, which stands for "Long-Term Evolution," is a standard for high-speed wireless communication that forms the basis of many 4G networks.

Reduced Latencies: 4G networks provided reduced latencies, which is essential for real-time applications such as video conferencing.

5. The Effects of New Technologies on Society and Culture

The development of mobile networks had an enormous effect, both technologically and socially, and continues to do so.

5.1. Recent Developments in Technology

One of the most visible changes brought about by technical progress was the miniaturization of electronic gadgets. Gone are the days of bulky, brick-like phones; in their place are sleek, pocket-sized devices.

Battery Life: Developments in battery technology have allowed for longer periods of continuous use.

Smartphones: The introduction of smartphones, which were made feasible by the availability of high-speed data and app stores, completely altered the way in which individuals use mobile devices.

Internet Access Via Mobile Devices The ubiquitous availability of internet access via mobile devices has completely disrupted traditional modes of information access, communication, and entertainment.

5.2. Alterations in Society

The advent of mobile technology has been a primary factor in the expansion of the economy, both in terms of job opportunities and overall business opportunities.

Connectivity on a Global Scale The global roaming capabilities of the second generation (2G) and the data services of later generations have connected individuals all over the world.

Mobile devices have become a vital part of daily life, having an impact on how we communicate, work, and shop, as well as how we socialize with one another.

In spite of the progress that has been made on a global scale, there is still a digital divide, which manifests itself in unequal access to mobile technology between urban and rural areas as well as between groups of high and low socioeconomic status.

6. Obstacles and Prospective Developments

The progression from 1G to 4G has been revolutionary, but it hasn't been without its share of difficulties.

6.1 Obstacles to Overcome

Spectrum Allocation: As the demand for data continues to rise, network operators will face increasing difficulty in distributing sufficient spectrum.

Network Security Due to the ever-increasing reliance on mobile networks, it is imperative that these networks maintain a high level of security in order to secure the data and privacy of their users.

Regulatory and Logistical Obstacles and Difficult Logistical Challenges Infrastructure Investment The development of advanced networks demands a considerable investment in infrastructure, which typically involves difficult regulatory and logistical obstacles.

Impact on the Environment: While mobile technology is a godsend in many ways, it also adds to the production of electronic trash and the consumption of energy, which prompts the need for sustainable solutions.

6.2. Forecasts of Future Trends

5G Technology: 5G is the next step in the evolution of mobile networks, promising even better speeds, lower latency, and greater connection. 5G is the abbreviation for the fifth generation. It is anticipated that it will power the Internet of Things as well as driverless vehicles.

Integration of AI: In the future, artificial intelligence will play an increasingly essential role in improving the performance of networks and enabling the development of new applications.

Edge Computing: The increased use of edge computing will lead to a reduction in latency, which will result in real-time applications that are more responsive and reliable.

Satellite Networks: The development of satellite networks has the potential to bring mobile connectivity to previously inaccessible regions and to provide dependable fallback options.

The progression from 1G to 4G in the world of mobile networks has been a fascinating one, one that has been distinguished by technological advancements, sociological transformations, and a seemingly endless supply of new prospects. The future of mobile networks is bright and holds the potential to further alter how we live, work, and communicate. With the introduction of 5G on the horizon and other developing technologies such as artificial intelligence and edge computing, the future of mobile networks is bright. The history of mobile networks is not even close to being finished, and they will continue to have a major impact on the world we live in.

1.2 What is 5G, and why is it a game-changer?

The introduction of 5G technology has ushered in a period of dramatic change within the context of the global telecoms industry. 5G, which is frequently referred to as the fifth generation of wireless technology, holds the potential to be a game-changer due to the revolutionary effect that it will have on connectivity. In the course of this investigation of 5G, we will look into what it is, how it works, and the reasons why it has the ability to change industries, improve our day-to-day lives, and pave the way for the Internet of Things (IoT).

1. Gaining an Understanding of 5G
   1.1. The development of wireless technology is discussed
   It is essential to know 5G's position in the progression of wireless technology in order to realize the significance of this new standard. The 1980s marked the beginning of mobile communication with the introduction of 1G (First Generation) analog cellular systems. The second generation (2G) brought about digital technology and SMS; the third generation (3G) brought about mobile data and internet access; and the fourth generation (4G) stretched data speeds and capabilities even further.

   The fifth-generation wireless communications standard, or 5G, is the most recent development in this line of work. It promises speeds that have never been seen before, low latency, and connection that extends beyond mobile devices to include a wide range of businesses and applications.

   1.2. The Principal Characteristics of 5G
   1.2.1 Rapidity and a Low Number of Latencies
   The remarkable speed that 5G may provide is one of its most notable characteristics. It provides peak data rates that can reach up to 20 Gbps, which is nearly 100 times faster than 4G's maximum speeds. This enables experiences that are both instantaneous when downloading and seamless while streaming. This speed is accompanied by extremely low latency, which can be as low as 1 millisecond. Real-time communication and apps rely heavily on low latency, which improves the fluidity and responsiveness of activities like online gaming and video conferencing.

   1.2.2 Extremely High Levels of Connectivity
   When compared to earlier generations, the 5G network is intended to be capable of supporting a much greater number of devices in a given space. This functionality is particularly critical for the Internet of Things (IoT), which will require seamless communication from billions of devices, ranging from smart appliances to industrial sensors. There is a possibility that 5G might support up to one million devices per square kilometer.

   1.2.3 Slicing of the Network
   The 5G technology will usher in a new era with its ability to slice networks. It grants operators the ability to establish several virtual

networks within the confines of a single physical infrastructure. Each individual virtual network, also known as a "slice," is capable of being adapted to meet the requirements of a particular use case, such as industrial automation, autonomous vehicles, or smart cities. Because of this customisation, resource allocation and service optimization may be accomplished efficiently.

2. The Foundational Elements of 5G Technology

To get a complete understanding of 5G, it is necessary to investigate the technological factors that are the foundation of this game-changing network.

2.1. Bands of Operating Frequencies

5G uses a much wider range of frequencies to transmit and receive data than its predecessors did. These frequency ranges can be divided, in a general sense, into two distinct bands:

2.1.1 Bands Below 6 GHz

The sub-6 GHz frequency spectrum is utilized by the majority of initial 5G deployments. Because it strikes a healthy balance between coverage and capacity, this band is well suited for use in both urban and suburban settings.

2.1.2 Millimeter Waves

Millimeter-wave spectrum, often known as mmWave spectrum, refers to frequencies that are higher than 24 GHz. It is the factor that enables 5G to achieve its potential of ultra-high speed and minimal latency. mmWave, on the other hand, has a shorter range and is more sensitive to interference from buildings and other barriers; as a result, it is generally utilized in metropolitan regions that have a high population density.

2.2. Beamforming

The technology known as beamforming is an essential component of 5G networks. Instead of broadcasting signals in a consistent manner in all directions, the network is able to concentrate its signal exactly on a particular user or device because to this capability. Even at mmWave frequencies, the signal's quality and dependability are improved as a result of this.

2.3. MIMO, which stands for "Multiple-Input, Multiple-Output

The technique known as Massive MIMO is essential to the functioning of 5G. It makes use of a large number of antennas in order to send and receive data, which considerably improves the network's capacity as well as its dependability. MIMO has the ability to adapt to changing conditions by dynamically directing signal beams to users. This helps to reduce interference and improves the performance of the network as a whole.

2.4. Core Network

The core network of 5G, also commonly referred to as the "5G Core," is planned to be more adaptable and scalable than previous generations' core networks. It supports a wide variety of services and applications and has a cloud-based architecture, which enables effective resource management and individualized service configuration.

2.5 The Virtualization of Networks

5G networks make use of techniques for network virtualization in order to build virtual network slices, each of which is customized to a different set of use cases. This makes it possible for operators to provide optimal services for a wide variety of sectors and applications, such as communication that is ultra-reliable and low-latency for autonomous vehicles or enormous IoT connections for smart cities.

3. Potential Uses for the New 5G Technology

The revolutionary potential of 5G extends across a wide range of business sectors as well as application domains.

3.1. Enhanced Mobile Broadband (also known as eMBB).

Enhanced Mobile Broadband (eMBB) is one of the key use cases for 5G. It provides significantly quicker download and upload rates, which substantially improves the user's experience when using mobile internet. Streaming video material in 4K and 8K resolution, as well as gaming and applications for augmented reality, become more immersive and accessible.

3.2. IoT (Internet of Things) comes in at number

By delivering dependable connectivity to a wide variety of connected devices, 5G is positioned to hasten the expansion of the Internet of Things (IoT). The Internet of Things, which includes anything from connected industrial machinery and smart cities to sensors used in healthcare and the environment, is poised to flourish with the advent of 5G.

3.3. Driverless Cars and Trucks

The low latency offered by 5G networks is an essential component for autonomous vehicles. It makes possible communication in real time between vehicles, infrastructure, and traffic control systems, making it possible for self-driving cars to function in a manner that is both safe and effective.

3.4 The Healthcare System

The rollout of 5G will make telemedicine and remote surgery more practicable. Real-time consultations, remote diagnostics, and even surgery that is carried out by specialists from a distance are all made possible because to the combination of high data transfer speeds and low latency.

3.5. The combination of Augmented and Virtual Reality (AR/VR)

The development of AR and VR experiences that are more immersive is made easier by 5G. Users are able to enjoy high-quality video without the lag or disconnection issues that have plagued earlier virtual reality experiences thanks to connectivity that is both high-speed and low-latency.

3.6. Intelligent Cities

The development of smart cities is greatly aided by the use of 5G. It enables real-time monitoring and optimization of public services and utilities, including traffic and utility systems. The end consequence is urban life that is more effective and environmentally friendly.

3.7. Automation in the Industrial Sector

The capacity of 5G to handle enormous Internet of Things connectivity is beneficial to the industrial industry. This results in more efficient processes, as it enables remote monitoring and control of machines, predictive maintenance, and the automation of large-scale tasks.

4. The Effects That 5G Will Have

The broad use of 5G technology has a variety of ramifications, some of which are beneficial while others provide challenges.

4.1. The Effect on the Economy

It is anticipated that the rollout of 5G networks will encourage economic growth by generating new job opportunities and openings within the technology sector. It will increase productivity across many different industries, which will further propel economic progress.

4.2. Concerns Regarding Safety

It is of the utmost importance to ensure the safety of these networks as 5G increasingly

becomes ingrained in both essential infrastructure and day-to-day activities. It is absolutely necessary to protect sensitive data as well as communications from cyber threats.

4.3. Concerns Regarding Privacy

Privacy concerns have been raised as a result of the growth of IoT devices connected over 5G. It is possible for this to result in the collecting of enormous amounts of personal data, which then begs the questions of how this information is utilized, stored, and safeguarded.

4.4. Investment in Physical Infrastructure

In order to roll out 5G infrastructure, significant investments need to be made in network equipment, spectrum acquisition, and regulatory compliance. This is a dilemma for some nations as well as the companies that provide network services.

4.5. The Impact on the Environment

The increased energy consumption of 5G infrastructure as well as the disposal of outdated equipment both have ramifications for the environment. To reduce the severity of this impact, it is absolutely necessary to develop sustainable solutions for 5G networks.

5. Obstacles and Potential Developments in the Future

The 5G technology will continue to develop over the next few years despite the many obstacles it must overcome.

5.1. Extent of Coverage and Distribution

It will be a huge task to ensure that 5G coverage is complete in all locations, including urban and rural ones. It requires the deployment of a significant amount of infrastructure, which can be a challenge both logistically and financially.

5.2. The Distribution of the Spectrum

To fully realize the promise of 5G, it is necessary to allocate spectrum in an effective manner. In order to guarantee that sufficient spectrum is accessible for all operators, there may be a need for regulatory adjustments as well as international collaboration.

5.3. Capability of Interoperation

It is of the utmost importance to ensure interoperability between the various 5G networks and devices. This guarantees that consumers will have seamless access to 5G services, even when travelling across different networks and areas.

5.4. Development toward 6G

Even as the 5G network is being rolled out, academics are actively investigating the possibilities presented by the 6G system. It is still hypothetical as to what the actual specifications of 6G will be, but it is anticipated that it will provide speeds that are even higher, lower latency, and accommodate applications that are much more inventive.

1.3 Key features of 5G technology

A substantial step forward has been taken in the field of telecommunications thanks to the introduction of the fifth generation of wireless technology, which is more generally referred to as 5G. It has a plethora of outstanding features that make it a game-changer in the digital age, and it promises to transform the way in which we connect with one another. During this in-depth investigation, we will delve into the primary characteristics of 5G technology and examine how those characteristics are reshaping connectivity.

1. Extremely Rapid Velocities
   The incredible speed of 5G technology is likely the characteristic that draws the most attention and is known to the most people. It is anticipated that 5G would transmit data rates as high as 20 Gbps, which is nearly 100 times faster than 4G's maximum speed. Users are able to engage in data-intensive activities such as downloading huge files, streaming high-definition videos, and playing data-intensive games without experiencing any visible lag or delay thanks to the quick data transmission rate. The need for buffering will become a thing of the past as such speeds bring in a new era of multimedia experiences that are uninterrupted.

   This functionality is notably helpful for applications such as augmented reality (AR) and virtual reality (VR), which require high-speed data in order to create experiences that are immersive and realistic. The latency experienced by online gamers is significantly reduced, and the process of streaming video content in 4K or 8K is made to be seamless and buffer-free.

2. Extremely Low Delay Times
   One of the most important aspects of wireless communication is called latency, and it refers to the amount of time it takes for data to move from its origin to its destination. The 5G network has extremely low latency, with delays as low as 1 millisecond. This is a game-changing feature, particularly for applications that require real-time communication and reaction. Specifically, this capability changes the game.

   In applications such as autonomous vehicles, where instant communication between vehicles, infrastructure, and traffic control systems is critical for safe and effective operation, low latency is essential. In the field of medicine, this permits remote surgeries and consultations thanks to the fact that medical professionals may carry out procedures with very little delay. In a similar vein, reduced latency enables immediate control and monitoring of machinery in industrial automation systems, which contributes to increased levels of both productivity and safety.

3. Connectivity for a Vast Amount of Devices
   When compared to earlier generations, the 5G network is intended to be capable of supporting a much greater number of devices in a given space. This functionality is particularly critical for the Internet of Things (IoT), which will require seamless communication for billions of devices. The fact that 5G has the capacity to support up to one million devices per square kilometer makes it ideally suited for Internet of Things (IoT) applications.

It is anticipated that the Internet of Things will change a variety of industries, including smart cities, healthcare, agriculture, and manufacturing. The vast device connectivity provided by 5G enables everything from smart appliances and environmental sensors to industrial equipment and autonomous drones to connect and communicate with one another in a seamless manner, which paves the way for more effective data collecting, monitoring, and automation.

4. Network Segmentation

The 5G technology will usher in a new era with its ability to slice networks. It gives the operators of a network the ability to build several virtual networks while utilizing the same physical infrastructure. Each individual virtual network, also known as a "slice," is capable of being adapted to meet the requirements of a particular use case, such as industrial automation, autonomous vehicles, or smart cities. Because of the customization, resource allocation and service optimization are both made more efficient.

The ability to slice a network is a particularly useful tool for meeting the varied requirements of a variety of applications. For instance, autonomous vehicles require connection that is low-latency and high-reliability, but smart cities require a network that is designed for connecting huge numbers of Internet of Things devices. By utilizing network slicing, operators are able to supply the specific services that are required for each application. This results in an overall improvement in the effectiveness and performance of the network.

5. Bands of Various Frequencies

5G uses a much wider range of frequencies to transmit and receive data than its predecessors did. These frequency ranges can be divided, in a general sense, into two distinct bands:

5.1. Below six gigahertz

The sub-6 GHz frequency spectrum is utilized by the majority of initial 5G deployments. Because it strikes a healthy balance between coverage and capacity, this band is well suited for use in both urban and suburban settings. Sub-6 GHz frequencies are able to more successfully penetrate structures and obstructions than higher frequencies do, ensuring that customers continue to have stable connectivity even while they are inside of a building.

5.2. Millimeter Wave, often known as mmWave

Millimeter-wave spectrum, also known as mmWave spectrum, makes use of higher frequencies,

particularly those that are greater than 24 GHz. These frequencies allow for incredibly fast data transfer rates and are the primary factor for 5G's remarkable performance in heavily populated urban areas. On the other hand, mmWave signals have a shorter range and are more likely to be disrupted by interference from buildings and other types of obstructions. In order to get the most of mmWave's potential, network operators need to install it in regions with high population densities and high levels of data consumption.

6. Forming of beams

The technology known as beamforming is an essential component of 5G networks. It enables the network to direct its signal specifically toward a user or device, rather than broadcasting signals in an even manner in all directions, which is made possible by this feature. Even at mmWave frequencies, the signal's quality and dependability are improved as a result of this.

Beamforming is a technique that improves the effectiveness of a network by lowering the amount of signal interference and focusing the signal toward the user. This results in a stronger and more reliable connection. This capability is particularly useful in urban situations because signals can easily be blocked by buildings and other obstructions in those settings.

7. MIMO, which stands for multiple-input and multiple-output.

The Massive Multiple-Input, Multiple-Output (MIMO) technology is an essential component of the 5G network. It makes use of a large number of antennas in order to send and receive data, which considerably improves the network's capacity as well as its dependability. The massively multiple input, multiple output, or MIMO, technology is what makes 5G's enormous data rates and enhanced signal quality a reality.

MIMO has the ability to adapt to changing conditions by dynamically directing signal beams to users. This helps to reduce interference and improves the performance of the network as a whole. It is an essential piece of technology that must be implemented in order to provide dependable connectivity in both urban and rural locations.

8. The Central Network

The core network of 5G, also commonly referred to as the "5G Core," is planned to be more adaptable and scalable than previous generations' core networks. It is able to support a wide variety of applications and services, which enables effective resource allocation and individualized service configuration. Because it is based on cloud computing, the architecture of the core network enables operators to deploy and manage services in a more dynamic manner, which makes it simpler to adjust to the ever-shifting requirements of users and applications.

9. the virtualization of networks

5G networks make use of techniques for network virtualization in order to build virtual network slices, each of which is customized to a different set of use cases. This enables operators to provide optimal services for a variety of industries and applications, including as highly dependable and low-latency communication for autonomous vehicles and vast Internet of Things connection for smart cities.

In addition to this, virtualization makes it possible to effectively allocate network resources, which in turn helps to save operating costs and improve network performance overall. It is an essential characteristic for guaranteeing that 5G will be able to satisfy the various demands posed by a wide variety of applications and sectors.

1.4 5G's impact on the telecom landscape

A new age has begun in the telecommunications industry with the introduction of 5G technology, which promises to transform the ways in which people connect to one another, communicate with one another, and consume data. 5G is poised to revolutionize the landscape of the telecom industry in ways that were previously imagined. 5G will have speeds that have never been seen before, lower latency, and larger capacity. In this article, we will investigate the multidimensional influence that 5G will have on the telecommunications industry. More specifically, we will investigate the implications that 5G will have for network infrastructure, consumer experiences, corporate applications, and the larger digital ecosystem.

Infrastructure Improvements for Networks

The effect that 5G will have on network infrastructure is one of the most significant repercussions it will have on the telecommunications industry. Small cell technology, which entails the deployment of multiple small, low-powered base stations throughout urban areas, serves as the basis upon which 5G networks are constructed. Because of the efficient utilization of higher-frequency spectrum made possible by these small cells, the network capacity was increased while congestion was decreased. As a consequence of this, 5G networks are able to accommodate the increased demand for data-intensive applications such as augmented reality, virtual reality, and Internet of Things (IoT) devices.

The migration to a 5G infrastructure will bring both difficulties and possibilities for telecommunications service providers. Although it needs large expenditures in new equipment and technology, it offers the possibility of new revenue streams through the sale of network access, infrastructure, and services; yet, it does require substantial investments in new equipment and technology. Because of this dynamic transition in infrastructure, the competitive environment of the telecommunications industry will be reshaped, and early adopters will have a considerable advantage.

Experiences Gained by Customers

It is impossible to emphasize how much of an impact 5G will have on the experiences of consumers. The unrivaled speed and low latency of 5G networks make it possible to stream videos in 4K and 8K resolutions without interruption, play online games without experiencing lag, and download enormous files in an instant. These advancements are not only applicable to the entertainment industry but also to healthcare, education, and labor that may be done remotely.

For instance, telemedicine consultations can be carried out with video of a higher quality and real-time monitoring, and students can take part in virtual classrooms without the need to worry about being interrupted.

The Internet of Things (IoT) will also benefit from the increased connectivity provided by 5G, which will make it possible for smart homes, cities, and industries to function more effectively. The overall user experience will improve as a result of improvements in the dependability and responsiveness of linked wearables, smart appliances, and self-driving cars.

Applications for Businesses

The disruptive effects of 5G will be seen throughout all sectors of the economy, including enterprises and industries. A new generation of apps and services that were previously impractical or even impossible to implement is now possible as a result of the decreased network latency and better network capabilities. For instance, the manufacturing, logistics, and agriculture industries can leverage the capabilities of 5G to implement real-time remote control of machines, automated supply chain management, and precision farming.

In the field of medicine, the rollout of 5G will make it easier to create the concept of remote surgery, in which doctors will be able to carry out treatments on patients located miles away using ultra-low latency video and control, as well as high-definition video. In addition, training, design, and simulation applications will see significant development in the use of augmented reality (AR), virtual reality (VR), and other similar technologies as the technology becomes more accessible and responsive.

The Expanded Scope of the Digital Ecosystem

The influence of 5G is not limited to telecom carriers and the clients they serve. To take advantage of the opportunities presented by 5G, the larger digital ecosystem, which includes content creators, app developers, and service providers, will need to undergo certain necessary changes. The increased capabilities of 5G networks will need streaming platforms to produce material of a greater quality than they currently do. App developers will create more immersive experiences using AR and VR technology, while businesses will develop novel solutions to take advantage of the potential of 5G in their operations.

The ecosystem that supports 5G will benefit greatly from cloud computing's participation. Edge computing, which involves processing data closer to the source, will become essential in lowering latency for real-time applications in the near future. The establishment of edge data centers by cloud providers as a means of providing support for 5G networks has resulted in the formation of a mutually beneficial connection between cloud and telecom providers.

Connectivity for Areas That Are Currently Underserved Rural and Other

In addition, 5G has the ability to close the digital divide by making high-speed internet access more widely available in rural and other underserved areas. The implementation of traditional wired infrastructure in these areas can be prohibitively expensive; but, the more compact cell sizes and wireless capabilities of 5G make it a more workable choice. This spread of 5G networks into previously disadvantaged areas has the potential to enable previously underserved groups to have access to economic opportunities, healthcare services, and online educational resources.

Concerns and Things to Take Into Account

Although the influence of 5G on the existing telecom environment holds a great deal of promise, there are a number of problems and factors to take into mind. The migration to 5G will need significant investments, including the creation of new infrastructure and the assignment of extra airwaves. In addition, there are worries regarding privacy and security, in particular in light of the expansion of Internet of Things devices and the possibility of cyberattacks on key infrastructure.

The deployment of 5G has also spurred discussions concerning the health impacts of increasing exposure to radiofrequency radiation, which has been sparked by the implementation of 5G. Although previous research has not produced any definitive evidence of danger, it is critical that continued research and public awareness initiatives be conducted to address these concerns.

A new era of connectivity, communication, and data consumption is about to begin thanks to the advent of 5G technology, which is set to completely transform the telecom sector. The increased network infrastructure of 5G, improved consumer experiences, innovative corporate applications, and broader ecosystem influence are some of the ways in which 5G promises to alter the way in which we engage with one another and with technology. It is vital for stakeholders to adapt, invest, and address obstacles in order to fully exploit the potential of this groundbreaking technology as 5G network development progresses. This can be accomplished by addressing the issues. 5G is the next generation of telecoms technology, and the revolutionary effects it will have on our digital world will be felt for many years to come.

Chapter 2

The Power of Cloud Computing

Cloud computing has quickly become recognized as one of the most revolutionary and game-changing technologies of the information age. It offers unparalleled levels of flexibility, scalability, and cost-effectiveness, and as a result, it has completely transformed the way in which individuals and corporations store, retrieve, and process data. During this in-depth investigation of the capabilities of cloud computing, we will investigate its origins, its fundamental ideas, the numerous advantages it offers to a variety of industries, the difficulties it presents, and the possibilities it holds for the future.

1. Acquiring Knowledge of Cloud Computing
   1.1. The Definitive Analysis and Central Ideas
   Cloud computing may be broken down into its component parts, the most fundamental of which is the technology that facilitates the delivery of computing services via the internet. These services can include servers, storage, databases, networking, software, analytics, and intelligence. When it comes to the management and storage of data, cloud computing gives users access to a huge network of remote servers that are housed on the internet. This eliminates the need to rely on a personal computer or a local server.
   The term "Infrastructure as a Service," or "IaaS," refers to the process of making virtualized computing resources available to customers via the internet. Users have the option to rent resources such as virtual computers, storage, and networking. Amazon Web Services (AWS), Microsoft Azure, and Google Cloud Platform are just a few examples of well-known IaaS providers.
   Platform as a Service (PaaS) is an offering that gives developers the

ability to build, deploy, and maintain applications without having to worry about the underlying infrastructure. PaaS provides a platform for this purpose. App Engine from Google and the Azure App Service from Microsoft are two good examples.

Software as a Service, also known as SaaS, is a model that gives customers access to various software applications through the usage of the internet.

Users can access these programs through a web browser; the third-party providers who host and maintain them are responsible for their upkeep. Applications like as Google Workspace, Microsoft 365, and Salesforce are examples of common SaaS programs.

1.2. The Development of Computing in the Cloud

The concept of cloud computing can be traced all the way back to the 1960s, when computer scientists and engineers conceived of a model for a system that would enable several users to share a single mainframe computer remotely. Cloud computing has its roots in this time period. The idea progressed over the course of several decades, but it wasn't until the early 2000s that cloud computing in the form that we are familiar with today began to take shape.

The introduction of Amazon Web Services (AWS) in 2002 represented a crucial turning point in the history of the development of cloud computing. AWS made it possible for businesses to remotely host their apps and services by providing the necessary infrastructure. Soon after that, a number of other significant competitors, including as Microsoft and Google, entered the market, which led to an intensification of competition and the acceleration of innovation.

The cloud has undergone continuous development thanks to the launch of numerous innovative services and technology. Because of this evolution, a wide variety of applications and use cases have been possible, including web hosting and data storage as well as artificial intelligence and machine learning.

2. The Many Advantages of Utilizing Cloud Computing

2.1. Reduction in Expenditures

The enormous cost reductions that may be realized through the utilization of cloud computing make this methodology an appealing choice for organizations of any size. In the past, considerable initial and ongoing financial investment was necessary for the installation and upkeep of infrastructure located on the premises. A pay-as-you-go model takes the place of these costs when using the cloud computing service. The capacity of an organization's resources can be increased or decreased on demand, saving the business the expense of maintaining unused gear. This resource-allocation methodology that is also cost-efficient allows both small startups and large organizations to better utilize their available resources.

In addition, cloud service providers take care of hardware maintenance, which eliminates the need for on-site information technology support and cuts operational expenses. Instead, businesses can direct their resources on the development of new products and services and the expansion of their operations.

2.2. Capacity for Growth and Adaptability

The scalability of cloud computing is one of the most significant advantages it offers. Whether they increase or decrease their resources, businesses are able to promptly adjust to changes in customer demand. This elasticity is especially useful in circumstances characterized by variable workloads or seasonal peaks in demand. For example, businesses that engage in online retail can easily scale their infrastructure during the busy holiday shopping season, thereby guaranteeing that their customers have a positive experience.

In addition, cloud computing gives users the freedom to experiment with different applications and technologies without the need to make major initial financial expenditures. This adaptability not only encourages innovation but also enables organizations to rapidly respond to shifts in the market.

2.3. Availability of Access and Collaborative Work

Users are able to access their data and applications through the use of cloud computing from nearly any location with an internet connection. This accessibility is particularly useful for remote work because it enables employees to work together on projects and gain access to essential information regardless of where they are physically located. Collaboration solutions hosted in the cloud, such as Google Workspace and Microsoft 365, have emerged as an essential component of today's successful enterprises.

In addition, the cloud makes it possible for numerous people to simultaneously collaborate on the same document or project. This type of real-time collaboration is made possible by the cloud. The increased productivity and streamlined workflows that result from this degree of collaboration are both impressive.

2.4 Safety and Contingency Planning for Unexpected Events

When people talk about cloud computing, they frequently bring up worries about security, yet the big cloud providers make substantial investments in security procedures, which frequently go beyond what many enterprises can accomplish on their own. These providers employ specialized teams of security professionals and make use of cutting-edge security technologies to keep customers' personal information safe.

The suppliers of cloud services also give comprehensive disaster recovery options. Typically, data is kept in a manner that is known as redundant storage across numerous data centers, which lowers the likelihood of losing data as a result of malfunctioning hardware or natural catastrophes. The resilience of the data is ensured by the presence of this redundancy as well as automated backup and recovery services.

2.5. Negative Effects on the Environment

The cloud has the potential to make the planet a more sustainable and environmentally friendly place. Cloud computing has the potential to drastically reduce energy usage since it can maximize the use of available resources and cut down on the demand for on-premises data centers. The usage of renewable energy sources is becoming an increasingly important emphasis for cloud service providers, which helps them reduce their carbon footprint even further.

The capability of the cloud to facilitate remote work has the potential to lessen the harmful effects on the environment that are caused by everyday commutes and office buildings. There can be a reduction in emissions of greenhouse gases if there are fewer commuters and smaller physical office spaces.

3. The Application of Cloud Computing in Businesses

3.1. Small and Medium-sized Businesses (often referred to as SMEs)

Computing in the cloud has leveled the playing field for small and medium-sized enterprises (SMEs), giving them access to the same technological and infrastructure resources as larger organizations without forcing them to bear the same financial burden. Small and medium-sized businesses (SMEs) have the ability to implement cloud solutions that are customized to meet their unique requirements, which enables them to scale as their businesses expand.

Numerous cloud-based software and solutions are designed specifically for small and medium-sized businesses (SMEs), and they offer crucial services such as customer relationship management (CRM), human resources, and accountancy. Consequently, small and medium-sized businesses are able to concentrate on their core skills while outsourcing their IT and administrative work.

In addition, the cloud has made it easier for small and medium-sized businesses to expand internationally. They have easy access to a customer base that spans the globe and are able to interact with partners and staff located all over the world.

3.2. Small Businesses and Startups

Cloud computing has been embraced by many large organizations in order to increase the effectiveness of their operations, efficiency, and innovation. Cloud computing enables these businesses to more effectively handle their huge data collections, which in turn enables them to make decisions and make forecasts based on the data.

E-commerce businesses, for instance, make use of data analytics carried out in the cloud in order to individualize their interactions with customers and improve the efficiency of their supply chain operations.

The scalability offered by the cloud is vital for huge organizations that must deal with fluctuating amounts of labor and traffic. They are able to handle peak demand without having to sacrifice performance or incurring unnecessary expenditures because to this capability.

In addition, cloud computing has made it possible for huge businesses to move away from archaic systems and toward cloud-native designs that are more flexible. This change encourages creativity, shortens the amount of time needed to bring new products and services to market, and enhances connection with customers.

4. Use of Cloud Computing in Public Organizations

4.1. The Administration

Cloud computing has been implemented by government agencies all around the world in an effort to improve the delivery of services, increase efficiency, and save costs. Cloud services make it possible for government organizations to update their information technology infrastructure while still adhering to stringent spending limits.

The way that governments manage and store huge volumes of data, for example, has been revolutionized as a result of cloud computing, which has ensured improved data security, accessibility, and compliance with regulatory standards. In addition, cloud computing solutions can be utilized to develop and manage electronic government services, which makes it simpler for individuals to gain access to vital services over the internet.

The technology of the cloud is also highly helpful in emergency situations and in recovering from them. The infrastructure of the cloud can be utilized by governments for the purposes of data backup, analysis of data in real time, and the coordination of emergency services in the event of a natural disaster or a public health emergency.

4.2. Instructional

The education industry has reaped significant benefits from cloud computing in recent years. The adoption of cloud-based learning management systems by educational institutions has made it possible to educate students remotely and online, which is especially important during the COVID-19 epidemic. These platforms make communication, material exchange, and the submission of assignments much easier to accomplish.

Because to cloud computing, educational resources are now more easily available and more cost-efficient. There is less of a need for physical materials now that students and teachers are able to access textbooks, videos, and interactive content from anywhere in the world. In addition, cloud-based collaboration tools encourage student connection as well as the creation of group projects.

5. Obstacles and Causes for Concern

   5.1. Safety and Personal Confidentiality

   When it comes to cloud computing, security continues to be one of the most pressing problems. Despite the significant investments made by cloud providers in the form of security measures, enterprises are still responsible for the safety of their own data. A breach can have serious repercussions, including the theft of data and damage to a company's brand.

   Encryption of data, identity and access management, and routine security audits are some of the best ways for enterprises to protect themselves from these threats and reduce the likelihood that they will be exploited. In addition, companies need to give careful consideration to the physical location of their data due to the fact that the legislation governing data compliance and data sovereignty differ from country to country.

   5.2. Issues Relating to Compliance and the Law

   It's possible that different regulatory and legal obligations could apply to data that's been stored in the cloud. Companies have a responsibility to ensure that their cloud service providers are in compliance with applicable legislation, such as the General Data Protection Regulation (GDPR) in Europe or HIPAA in the United States. Should you fail to comply, you risk incurring significant penalties.

   It is critical for enterprises to have a thorough understanding of their responsibilities and to devise data governance policies that are in line with the specific compliance requirements of their respective industries. For this purpose, close collaboration with legal and compliance professionals is frequently required.

   5.3. Unavailability of the Service and Its Dependability

   Outages in the cloud can cause severe problems for business operations and result in significant financial losses. Although most large cloud service providers guarantee high levels of availability and redundancy, no system is completely safe from experiencing outages from time to time.

Organizations can mitigate the effects of downtime by using multi-cloud or hybrid cloud strategies, which involve diversifying both the cloud service providers they use and the resources they keep on-premises. They should also build comprehensive disaster recovery plans in order to secure the continuity of their business in the event that services are interrupted.

6. The Prospects for Computing in the Cloud

6.1. Computing at the Edge

Computing at the network's edge is a developing trend that works in tandem with cloud computing. It includes processing data in a location that is physically closer to its origin, which helps to reduce latency and improve real-time performance. Computing at the edge is especially useful for applications such as driverless vehicles, Internet of Things devices, and industrial automation, in which the ability to make decisions in real time is essential.

An approach to data processing that is both more thorough and more efficient can be achieved by combining cloud computing with edge computing. In order to make the most of the opportunities presented by their data, organizations will need to integrate both perspectives.

6.2. Computing on the Quantum Level

The advent of computers based on quantum mechanics marks the beginning of a new era in the

field of computer technology. Quantum computing, despite the fact that it is still in its infancy, has the potential to transform the way data processing and encryption are done. Quantum computers have the potential to greatly accelerate difficult calculations, which would aid a variety of sectors including the search for new drugs, the study of new materials, and cryptography.

Cloud service companies are already investigating quantum computing services in the hopes of providing users with access to very advanced but yet relatively new computers.

6.3. Considerations of an Ethical Nature

As the significance of cloud computing continues to extend across a variety of fields, ethical questions are becoming an increasingly essential part of the conversation. At the heart of contemporary ethical debates are issues about data privacy, surveillance, and the appropriate application of artificial intelligence and machine learning.

In the not too distant future, businesses and cloud service providers will be required to address these concerns, put in place ethical frameworks, and guarantee openness and accountability in their utilization of technology.

The way in which we may store data, as well as access it and process it, has been revolutionized by cloud computing. Both the tremendous benefits it delivers to organizations, governments, and educational institutions, on the one hand, and the obstacles it causes, such as security and compliance issues, on the other, are evidence of the power that it possesses to be disruptive. With the development of edge computing, the introduction of quantum computing, and a greater emphasis on ethical considerations, the future of cloud computing holds enormous possibilities.

Cloud computing will continue to be an essential component of innovation even as the digital landscape undergoes further transformation. This will enable businesses to prosper in a world that is becoming increasingly data-driven and networked. Adopting cloud computing and finding solutions to the problems it poses is going to be absolutely necessary in order to maintain a competitive advantage and propel forward progress in the era of digital technology.

2.1 Evolution of cloud computing

Since its early conceptualization, cloud computing has undergone a remarkable evolution, becoming a revolutionary and fundamental component of the current digital world in the process. In the course of this investigation into the past of cloud computing, we are going to investigate its beginnings, as well as the major milestones and important breakthroughs that have helped to mold it into the potent technology that it is today.

Concepts that Came Before the Cloud and Its Ancestors
Where Did the Term "Cloud Computing" Come From?

The field of telecommunications is where the concept of "cloud computing" first gained traction. It wasn't until the 1960s that telecommunications corporations started use cloud symbols to describe network diagrams, which is when the term was first used. These cloud symbols symbolized aspects of the network that were out of the individual user's sphere of control.

The idea progressed over time to incorporate the provision of computing resources over a network, analogous to the manner in which telephone services were made available. This was accomplished by analogy with the provision of telephone services. This established the conceptual groundwork for cloud computing in its modern form that we are familiar with today.

Computing through Utility and Computing Through the Grid

Utility computing and grid computing are two examples of the kinds of ideas that helped pave the way for the creation of cloud computing.

The idea behind utility computing was to provide computing resources to users in the same way that utilities such as electricity or water are provided to people. Access to computing power on demand could be provided to companies and people, freeing them from the responsibility of owning and maintaining their own servers. This concept was brought to the forefront in the 1960s by John McCarthy, who is also credited with having an impact on the evolution of cloud computing services.

Computing on a Grid: This type of computing is based on the concept of delegating individual computing jobs to a number of different computers in order to solve more complicated issues. It was the first time that the idea of sharing resources across a network had been considered, which is one of the core aspects of cloud computing.

The Beginnings of Cloud Computing as We Know It

AWS stands for Amazon Web Services.

The early 2000s marked the beginning of the contemporary era of cloud computing, which was ushered in with the establishment of Amazon Web Services (AWS) in the year 2002. Infrastructure as a Service (IaaS) came into being when Amazon Web Services (AWS) made it possible for companies to rent computer power and storage space via the internet. This change revolutionized the way organizations saw their IT infrastructure and gave them the ability to scale their resources according to their needs without having to make significant financial commitments.

(GCP) stands for the Google Cloud Platform.

In 2008, Google introduced a product called Google App Engine, marking the company's entry into the cloud computing market. It was possible for developers to construct and host web applications using this platform. It was one of the original offers of Platform as a Service (PaaS), which aimed to simplify and abstract the management of infrastructure so that developers could concentrate on writing code instead.

Azure from Microsoft

2010 saw the launch of Microsoft Azure, an all-encompassing cloud computing platform that was developed by Microsoft. Azure made it possible for companies to create, deploy, and manage applications and services by utilizing Microsoft's extensive network of data centers located around the world. It provided a variety of services, such as IaaS, PaaS, and SaaS for its customers.

The Accelerating Growth of Cloud Services

IaaS stands for "infrastructure as a service."

Users are able to rent virtualized computing resources, such as servers, storage, and networking, while using IaaS, which is demonstrated by

Amazon Web Services (AWS), Microsoft Azure, and Google Cloud. It offers the fundamental stepping stones that are required for the development of several cloud-based apps and services.

PaaS stands for "platform as a service."

PaaS isolates infrastructure management, as shown by Google App Engine and Azure App Service. This enables developers to concentrate on designing and delivering apps rather than worrying about server provisioning and maintenance.

Software as a Service, sometimes known as "SaaS,"

The Software as a Service (SaaS) paradigm of cloud computing is considered to be the user-centric one. Users have access to software applications such as Google Workspace, Microsoft 365, and Salesforce over the internet. These applications are offered by the company. The accessibility and utilization of software in enterprises and by consumers has been revolutionized as a result of the rise of SaaS.

The Influence That Cloud Computing Will Have On Businesses And Technologies

Scalability and effective use of resources

The scalability of cloud computing has been extremely useful in assisting organizations in better managing their variable workloads. It enables enterprises to scale up or down according on their requirements, hence lowering the need for expensive hardware that is sitting idle. Because of this flexibility, organizations of all sizes have been able to realize significant cost reductions.

Traditional information technology models being upended

Cloud computing has caused traditional methods of information technology to become obsolete. By utilizing cloud services rather than maintaining their own on-premises data centers, organizations can cut down on the amount of internal IT assistance they require, hence reducing their overall operational costs. As a result of this disruption, both tiny companies and huge enterprises have gained influence.

Innovation and Digital Transformation Capabilities Enablement

Computing on the cloud has ushered in a new period of rapid technological advancement. It has been crucial in the development of upcoming technologies such as artificial intelligence, machine learning, and the Internet of Things (IoT). In addition to this, it has encouraged digital transformation, which has made it possible for companies to rethink their procedures, services, and overall consumer experiences.

The Obstacles in Our Way and the Way Forward

Concerns Regarding Both Security and Privacy

Despite the significant investments made by cloud providers in various security measures, there are still issues around security and privacy. To reduce the likelihood of adverse outcomes, businesses need to institute stringent security measures, which should include data encryption and identity management. Challenges also arise with regard to the sovereignty of data and compliance rules.

Cloud computing's Bright Future and Emerging Trends in the Industry

Emerging trends, such as the ones listed below, will shape the future of cloud computing.

Edge computing is the processing of data at a location closer to its source in order to improve real-time performance and decrease latency.

Computing on a quantum level has the ability to completely change how data is processed and encrypted.

Addressing concerns with data privacy, surveillance, and the responsible application of developing technology are examples of ethical considerations.

The development of cloud computing from its earliest conceptions to its most cutting-edge technologies has fundamentally altered the manner in which we access and manage data as well as computing resources. It has caused old forms of information technology to become obsolete, given firms scalability and the capacity to save money, and fostered innovation across a variety of industries.

The future of cloud computing has an incredible amount of promise, despite the continued existence of obstacles such as security and privacy concerns. The road forward is being shaped by developing trends such as edge computing and quantum computing, in addition to a heightened focus on ethical considerations. Computing on the cloud will continue to be an essential component of the digital transformation that is taking place in our world.

2.2 Types of cloud services (IaaS, PaaS, SaaS)

Cloud computing has completely altered the manner in which individuals and corporations gain access to and make use of computing resources. The three main categories of cloud services—Infrastructure as a Service (IaaS), Platform as a Service (PaaS), and Software as a Service (SaaS)—have been instrumental in the transformation of how technology is distributed, managed, and utilized. In this all-encompassing discussion, we will look into the unique qualities, functionalities, and applications of each kind of cloud service.

IaaS stands for "infrastructure as a service."

IaaS stands for "infrastructure as a service." is one of the fundamental pillars of cloud computing, as it gives users access to virtualized computer resources through the usage of the internet. It makes it possible to deploy and administer applications without having to make an investment in local hardware by providing the fundamental building blocks that are required for doing so. Users are able to construct and manage their own IT infrastructures by renting virtual servers, storage, and networking resources from cloud providers with the help of Infrastructure as a Service (IaaS).

Scalability is a feature of IaaS that enables customers to rapidly adjust the amount of computing resources they consume to meet their specific requirements. This helps users ensure that they have the capacity to deal with changing levels of work.

IaaS provides cost savings by removing the requirement for organizations to make initial investments in hardware and infrastructure upkeep. As a result, businesses are able to pay for the resources they use on a pay-as-you-go basis, which results in increased efficiency.

Users have more control over their own information technology environments thanks to increased flexibility, which allows them to select the operating systems, applications, and development platforms that best suit their needs.

Examples of Use Cases for IaaS:

IaaS provides developers with the required resources to design, test, and deploy applications without the need to make an investment in physical hardware. These resources include development and testing environments.

Website Hosting: Companies can utilize infrastructure as a service (IaaS) to host their websites and web applications, which ensures that they have the computational power and storage space required to manage web traffic.

PaaS stands for "platform as a service."

Providers of "Platform as a Service" provides a platform that simplifies the process of developing, testing, deploying, and managing applications by including infrastructure, middleware, and development tools. This simplifies the process of developing, testing, deploying, and managing applications. PaaS frees developers from the burden of worrying about the underlying infrastructure, allowing them to direct their attention solely to the creation of applications. It provides a framework that simplifies the process of application development and speeds up the time it takes to bring new apps to market.

Application Development Tools PaaS provides developers with a wide variety of development tools, which may include programming languages, libraries, and frameworks. These tools make it possible for developers to construct and deploy apps in a more time and effort effective manner.

Automatic Scaling: PaaS platforms have the ability to automatically scale applications based on demand, ensuring that applications are able to handle unexpected spikes in traffic without any intervention from a human being.

PaaS is able to improve cooperation among development teams by offering tools for version control, code sharing, and real-time collaboration. This enables development teams to work together more efficiently.

Examples of Uses for PaaS:

PaaS is extensively used for building and delivering web applications, mobile applications, and APIs. This enables developers to concentrate on coding rather than managing the underlying infrastructure, which frees up more time for them to work on their applications.

PaaS provides tools for data analytics and business intelligence, which enables enterprises to extract insights from enormous datasets and make decisions based on the data collected.

Software as a Service, sometimes known as "SaaS,"

Software as a Service (SaaS) is a model for delivering software applications to customers on a subscription basis over the internet. Users have access to and can make use of programs using a web browser while utilizing SaaS, eliminating the requirement for users to install or maintain software on their local devices. The use of software as a service (SaaS), which provides users with access to a variety of applications for both personal and professional use, has seen a rise in popularity in a number of different markets.

Accessibility: Software as a service (SaaS) programs can be used from any device as long as it has a web browser and an internet connection. This gives consumers the ability to access their software from any location.

Automatic Updates and Maintenance Because SaaS providers manage software updates and maintenance, users are guaranteed to always have access to the most recent features and security fixes with no further effort required on their part.

Subscription Model: Software as a service (SaaS) uses a pricing model that is based on subscriptions rather than one-time sales or long-term commitments. This model enables users to pay for software on a regular basis without the need for consumers to make any upfront purchases or obligations.

Examples of How SaaS Can Be Used

Tools for Productivity and Collaboration SaaS vendors typically offer a wide variety of tools for productivity and collaboration, such as email, document editing, project management, and communication tools.

SaaS-based CRM software allow firms to manage customer interactions, measure revenues, and automate marketing efforts. Customer

Relationship Management (CRM) is an acronym for "customer relationship management."

2.3 Cloud computing benefits for telecom

Cloud computing has had a significant influence on the telecommunications business, which is responsible for the infrastructure of communication on a global scale. The use of cloud computing has resulted in a plethora of benefits, one of which is a revolution in the way in which telecom firms operate, provide services, and attend to the needs of their consumers. In this piece, we will discuss the enormous benefits that cloud computing offers the telecommunications industry as well as the ways in which it is altering the environment.

1. Reductions in expenses and gains in productivity

   The ability to save money is one of the most immediate and obvious benefits that cloud computing may provide for the telecommunications business. Historically, telecommunications businesses were required to make significant financial investments in the construction and upkeep of substantial physical infrastructure, which included data centers, servers, and network equipment. These companies have the potential to dramatically lower their capital expenditures as well as their operations costs by utilizing cloud computing.

   By switching to services that are hosted in the cloud, telecommunications companies can avoid the need to construct and maintain their own data centers, which saves money on the costs of real estate, power, and cooling, as well as on the costs of hiring qualified staff. This change to an OpEx model enables businesses to pay for resources on an as-needed basis, which enables them to make the most of their available financial resources.

2. Capacity for Growth and Adaptability

   The telecommunications business is subject to shifting demand, particularly in the wake of unforeseen occurrences such as natural disasters, unique events, or abrupt increases in user traffic. Cloud computing gives telecom firms the ability to instantly scale up or down their resource allocation in response to changing demand. Because of this elasticity, they are able to supply their consumers with services that are both uninterrupted and of a high quality.

   Cloud computing enables telecom companies to swiftly introduce new services and expand existing ones, allowing them to more effectively respond to shifting market conditions and evolving client requirements. Cloud computing gives businesses the flexibility they need to maintain their competitive edge in an industry that is undergoing rapid change. This flexibility can be used to increase network capacity, add new features, or launch novel services.

3. The Optimization and Performance of the Network

   Cloud computing gives telecommunications firms access to the tools and the infrastructure they need to improve the performance of their networks. When operators make use of cloud-based network functions, such as Network Function Virtualization (NFV) and Software-Defined Networking (SDN), they are able to improve the effectiveness of their networks, cut down on network latency, and guarantee their clients a greater quality of service.

   In addition, cloud-based solutions make it easier to implement edge computing, which in turn

   enables telecom businesses to process data in a location that is physically closer to its origin. This brings down the latency, making it possible for real-time applications, such as augmented and virtual reality, to run across telecommunications networks. Edge computing also gives telecom carriers the ability to provide low-latency services, which are an essential element of applications such as autonomous vehicles and smart cities.

4. Increased Safety and Protection of Private Information

   Given the large amounts of sensitive data that are managed by companies in the telecom

   industry, security is an issue of the utmost importance. The suppliers of cloud computing services understand the need of taking stringent precautions to protect their customers' data and infrastructure, and as a result, they invest significantly in these areas. The data protection efforts of telecom businesses can benefit from the knowledge of cloud providers in the field of information security.

   A large number of cloud providers offer security features like as encryption, identity and access control, and compliance certifications. These services assist telecommunications firms in meeting regulatory requirements and protecting their customers' data. When it comes to data protection, the cloud's centralized and carefully managed security solutions can frequently outperform the safeguards that individual telecom firms can put in place on their own.

5. Reduced Time to Market and Accelerated Innovation

   In the telecommunications sector, quick innovation and the ongoing development of new

   technologies are two of the industry's defining characteristics. Computing in the cloud quickens the pace of innovation by offering a platform on which telecom operators can more quickly experiment with and introduce brand new services and features. Telecom firms can shorten the amount of time it takes to bring new products to market if they use infrastructure and development tools that are hosted in the cloud.In addition to this, cloud computing makes it easier for groups of people to work together, including teams, partners, and third-party developers. Because they can draw on a larger reservoir of expertise and resources, telecom businesses thrive in this collaborative atmosphere, which encourages innovation. Additionally, it fosters the creation of new apps and services, which is vital for maintaining a competitive advantage and satisfying the ever-changing demands of customers.

6. Enhancement of the Experiences of the Customers

The use of cloud computing can improve the user experience in a number of different ways. It enables telecom providers to offer novel services and applications that increase the user experience. Some examples of these are the ability to stream high-definition video and applications that utilize augmented reality. These services frequently demand a significant amount of computer power, which is conveniently provided by the cloud.

In addition, the adaptability of cloud computing makes it possible to integrate apps that deal directly with customers in a seamless manner. Customers will be able to benefit from a unified experience across a variety of devices and platforms as a result of this. Cloud technology helps telecom operators to provide a streamlined and dependable customer experience across a variety of use cases, including account management, content access, and the utilization of communication services.

7. A shorter time to recovery and increased resilience to natural disasters

The telecommunications business is susceptible to suffering huge losses in the event of natural disasters or malfunctioning networks. The use of cloud computing improves the capability to recover from natural disasters by providing choices for data redundancy, automatic backups, and geo-replication. It is possible to quickly restore essential data and services even in the case of an outage at the data center or a network breakdown.

In addition, the decentralized nature of cloud computing means that telecom companies are not reliant on a single data center or physical location for their operations. Because of this redundancy's contribution to the network's resilience, operators are able to keep the network available even when faced with challenging circumstances, such as natural catastrophes or cyberattacks.

8. Operations that are Sustainable

Computing in the cloud has an influence on the environment that is consistent with the increased emphasis on sustainability in the telecommunications business. The fact that cloud companies are increasingly turning to renewable energy sources to power their data centers has the effect of making cloud computing less harmful to the environment. Telecom businesses may lessen their impact on the environment and help move the world closer to a more sustainable future by migrating some of their infrastructure to the cloud.

In addition, the cloud enables working remotely and collaborating remotely, which eliminates the requirement for costly office buildings and the need to commute everyday.

This trend toward working from home helps to reduce emissions of greenhouse gases, an important aspect to take into account in today's society, which is more concerned about its impact on the environment.

The telecommunications sector has benefited greatly from the advent of cloud computing in a variety of ways. These benefits include cost reductions, scalability, network optimization, security, innovation, improved consumer experiences, resilience against natural disasters, and sustainability. The technology of the cloud gives telecom operators the ability to adapt to the ever-changing digital world, fulfill the demands of their customers, and stimulate innovation within the industry.

To ensure that it continues to be at the forefront of digital communication and connectivity, the telecommunications industry will be well-positioned to exploit the full potential of this technology as cloud computing continues to develop and mature.

Chapter 3

Convergence of 5G and Cloud

The introduction of fifth-generation wireless (5G) networks and cloud computing heralds a huge transition in technology that is on the cusp of reshaping the ways in which we communicate, work, and engage with the digital world. This convergence not only brings about mobile connectivity that is faster and more dependable, but it also offers a level of flexibility and scalability in cloud-based services that has never been seen before. During this in-depth examination of the convergence of 5G technology and cloud computing, we will delve into the fundamentals of 5G technology as well as the fundamental ideas of cloud computing. We will also discuss the synergies that exist between the two as well as the far-reaching ramifications that these developments will have on a variety of different businesses and fields.

Acquiring Knowledge of 5G

The introduction of 5G, the fifth generation of mobile network technology, will bring about a significant change in the ways in which people connect with one another and exchange information. It is not just an incremental enhancement over 4G; rather, it marks a paradigm shift in wireless communication and is a revolutionary step forward.

Introduction to the 5G System

When compared to its predecessors, 5G technology should be able to deliver significantly increased data transfer speeds, decreased latency, increased network capacity, and greater dependability. The implementation of 5G networks requires a variety of technological developments, such as the utilization of new radio frequencies, the implementation of huge Multiple Input Multiple Output (MIMO) systems, and network slicing, which enables network resources to be dynamically allocated to a variety of applications.

Key Characteristics of 5G:

Enhanced Data transmission Rates: 5G networks offer much higher data transmission rates, with speeds that can exceed 1 Gbps. This makes it possible to quickly download and upload huge files, stream ultra-high-definition video, and use applications in real time.

Reduced Latencies: One of the goals of 5G is to reduce latencies to one millisecond or less. This would make it perfect for applications that require real-time reactions, such as augmented reality (AR), virtual reality (VR), driverless vehicles, and remote surgery.

The term "network slicing" refers to a feature that gives network operators the ability to break their networks into many virtual networks, each of which is optimized for a different set of use cases. It guarantees that resources are assigned in an effective manner in accordance with the requirements of the various applications.

Investigating the Concept of the Cloud

Cloud computing is a game-changing technology that has altered the way in which individuals and corporations access, store, and analyze data. It is the process of providing consumers with computing services through the usage of the internet and provides users with flexibility, scalability, and cost-effectiveness.

Definition as well as Central Ideas

Cloud computing can be broken down into its most basic component, which is the provision of several computing services via the internet. These services include not only servers and storage but also databases, networking, software, and analytics, amongst other things. Users are able to gain access to and make use of these services without the necessity of locally installed hardware or infrastructure.

The following are some key concepts of cloud computing:

On-Demand Service: Cloud services are available on-demand, which enables customers to access resources and applications as needed, frequently on a pay-as-you-go basis. Cloud services are also known as utility computing or internet computing.

Pooling available resources and sharing them with several clients is a service that cloud providers offer. Through the pooling of resources, both cost savings and improved resource use are made possible.

Scalability is the ability of cloud resources to swiftly scale up or down, which enables businesses to adapt their operations to changing workloads and requirements.

Different Categories of Cloud Services

Infrastructure as a Service (IaaS) is a model that makes it possible for customers to rent servers, storage space, and networking capabilities. IaaS delivers virtualized computing resources to users via the internet.

Amazon Web Services (AWS), Microsoft Azure, and Google Cloud Platform (GCP) are three of the most notable IaaS providers currently available.

PaaS stands for "platform as a service," and it refers to a service that provides a platform that simplifies the process of application development, deployment, and management. Developers are free to concentrate on code and the logic of applications because the underlying infrastructure is hidden from them. App Engine from Google and the Azure App Service from Microsoft are two good examples.

Software as a Service, also known as SaaS, is the distribution of software applications through the use of the internet. Users are able to access these programs through their web browsers since they are hosted and managed by external service providers. Google Workspace, Microsoft 365, and Salesforce are a few examples of popular alternatives.

Combining 5G wireless technology with cloud computing

The convergence of fifth-generation (5G) wireless networking with cloud computing is not only the coexistence of two technologies; rather, it is a fundamental integration that capitalizes on the capabilities of both in order to establish a new standard for connectivity and computing.

The Improvements That 5G Will Bring to Cloud Computing

Transfer of Data at a Rapid Pace The fast data transfer speeds offered by 5G make it possible to quickly upload and download data from the cloud. This not only improves the experience for the user but also helps apps that rely on having real-time access to the resources stored in the cloud.

Low Latency: As a result of 5G's low latency, cloud apps will be able to respond to user inputs in a manner that is nearly immediate. This is essential for applications such as augmented reality (AR), virtual reality (VR), and driverless cars, in which even the smallest delay might have negative consequences.

Edge Computing: 5G makes edge computing possible, which is a method in which data is processed nearer to its point of origin. This eliminates the requirement for data to be transmitted to and from far-off data centers. This ultimately leads to quicker answers and a more effective utilization of the cloud's resources.

Network Slicing: The network slicing feature of 5G makes it possible for cloud providers to dynamically assign network resources in order to make them more suitable for a variety of applications. This ensures that essential applications, such as those used in healthcare or autonomous vehicles, acquire the required network resources in a timely manner.

The Role of Cloud Computing in Making 5G Possible

The infrastructure required to support the quick development and scaling of 5G networks is provided by cloud computing, which also offers the scalability and flexibility that comes along with it. The dynamic needs of 5G networks are ideally matched by the flexibility offered by cloud resources, which can be supplied and deprovisioned on demand.

Cloud-based network functions, such as Network Function Virtualization (NFV) and Software-Defined Networking (SDN), make it possible to optimize the use of network resources and distribute them in an effective manner. This efficiency applies to the provisioning of resources. This results in cost savings as well as enhanced performance for the network.

Automation and Orchestration: The use of cloud computing makes it possible to automate and orchestrate the functions of a network, which in turn simplifies the management and deployment of 5G services. The effectiveness of the network operations is improved as a result of this automation.

Effects on a Wide Range of Industries

The combination of fifth-generation mobile networks and cloud computing will have significant repercussions for a wide range of businesses and markets.

The field of telecommunications

This convergence results in greater network capabilities, more efficient resource allocation, and higher network performance for the telecoms sector as a whole. It is possible for telecom operators to provide their consumers with a larger variety of services and applications, which opens the door to new revenue streams. In addition, the implementation of edge computing enables telecom carriers to deliver low-latency services, which broadens the availability of real-time applications such as augmented reality (AR), virtual reality (VR), and online gaming.

Concerning medical care

Convergence of 5G wireless networking with cloud computing presents an opportunity for the development of game-changing solutions in the medical field. Real-time monitoring, telesurgery, and other forms of remote medical treatment are all capable of being carried out with high dependability and low latency. This facilitates the transmission of essential medical data in a secure manner and without delay.

Industrial Production

The manufacturing sector is positioned to reap the benefits of this convergence through the

adoption of Internet of Things (IoT) devices connected to 5G networks and data analytics performed in the cloud. By leveraging real-time data from their factories and supply networks, manufacturers may improve product quality, optimize production processes, and reduce the amount of time their production lines are down.

IoT stands for the Internet of Things.

IoT applications will benefit immensely from the combination of 5G and cloud computing. In combination with the processing power of the cloud, the high bandwidth, low latency, and scalable characteristics of 5G networks make it possible to connect and manage an enormous number of Internet of Things devices in an effective manner. This is absolutely necessary for smart cities, smart homes, industrial IoT, and a variety of other applications.

Vehicles that Drive Themselves

The development and implementation of autonomous vehicles are both dependent upon the convergence of 5G wireless technology and cloud computing. Because of the reduced latency of 5G networks, it will be possible for vehicles to communicate with one another and with the infrastructure that supports traffic in real time. Meanwhile, resources hosted in the cloud are able to collect and analyze massive volumes of data generated by sensors and cameras, making it possible for autonomous vehicles to operate in a manner that is both safe and effective.

Concerns and Things to Take Into Account

Safety and Confidentiality

The increasing connectivity and data flow that this convergence enables imposes a necessity for comprehensive security measures to be put into place. The protection of sensitive data, the maintenance of users' privacy, and the prevention of attacks via cyberspace are of the utmost importance.

Management of the Network

The management of intricate 5G networks and cloud resources calls for sophisticated technologies and extensive experience. In order to assure optimal performance, network operators need to make investments in knowledgeable staff as well as sophisticated management tools.

Concerns Relating to Regulations and Compliance

The convergence may present difficulties in regulatory and compliance matters, particularly in sectors such as the healthcare and financial industries. It is absolutely necessary to ensure compliance with all data protection legislation, standards, and government policies.

Influence on the Environment

The proliferation of 5G networks and cloud computing raises a number of environmental concerns, including the need for increased energy usage and better management of electronic trash. It is critical to engage in activities that are helpful to the environment.

The introduction of 5G networks and cloud computing will bring about a revolutionary change in the ways in which we connect with one another, interact with one another, and conduct business. This convergence of high-speed, low-latency mobile networks with scalable, flexible cloud resources offers up a world of options for a variety of industries, including telecommunications, healthcare, manufacturing, the internet of things, and autonomous cars, amongst others.

Despite the fact that there are significant benefits, there are also obstacles, particularly in the areas of security and privacy, which call for vigilance and creativity. This convergence, which is still developing, holds the promise of altering the way in which we live, work, and enjoy the digital world by providing us with new levels of connectivity and computational power.

3.1 How 5G and cloud technologies complement each other

Connectivity, communication, and computing are all undergoing profound shifts as a result of the powerful synergy created by the convergence of 5G and cloud technologies. While 5G will completely transform the capabilities of mobile networks, cloud technologies will give resources that are scalable and adaptable for use in apps and services. In this piece, we will investigate how the 5G and cloud technologies might work together to usher in a new era that is characterized by increased levels of innovation and connectedness.

The Development of 5G Networks

It is vital to have an understanding of what 5G technology is and the fundamental characteristics it possesses before delving into the ways in which it complements cloud computing.

Enhanced Data Transfer Rates: In comparison to 4G networks, data transfer rates on 5G networks are significantly higher. Users will be able to experience brisk downloads and uploads of material because of the possibility for data rates of many gigabits per second.

Reduced Latencies: One of the goals of 5G is to reduce latencies to one millisecond or less. This will make it possible for real-time interactions and applications that demand nearly instantaneous answers.

Network Slicing: The network slicing feature of 5G enables network operators to partition their physical networks into several virtual networks, each of which is tailored to meet the requirements of a particular application. Because of this, mission-critical applications are guaranteed to obtain the real-time network resources they demand.

Acquiring Knowledge on Cloud Computing Technologies

The supply of computing services via the internet is at the heart of cloud technologies, which, on the other hand, focus on the cloud. Cloud computing allows customers to access a wide variety of services, such as servers, storage, databases, networking, software, analytics, and more, without the need for local hardware or infrastructure in their own locations.

The following are important ideas related to cloud computing:

On-Demand Service: Cloud services are available on-demand, which enables customers to access resources and applications on-demand, frequently on a pay-as-you-go basis. Cloud services are also known as utility computing or internet computing.

Pooling of Resources: In cloud computing, providers pool and share their resources with several clients in order to achieve greater resource utilization and lower overall costs.

Scalability is the ability of cloud resources to swiftly scale up or down, which enables businesses to adapt their operations to changing workloads and requirements.

Each Other in a Complementary Manner

Both 5G and cloud technologies have their own distinct advantages, which allow them to overcome the shortcomings of the other. This creates a complementary relationship between the two.

The Improvements That 5G Will Bring to Cloud Computing

Transferring Data at a Rapid Pace: Compared to older generations of wireless technology, 5G networks are capable of moving data at a rate that is noticeably faster. This is especially helpful for cloud applications that require the uploading and downloading of data in a quick and efficient manner. Users are able to quickly access and manipulate big files stored in the cloud, which contributes to the increased efficacy and responsiveness of cloud-based services.

reduced Latency The reduced latency of 5G will be a game-changer for applications that run in the cloud. It enables real-time interactions with the resources that are hosted in the cloud, which makes it possible for applications such as augmented reality (AR), virtual reality (VR), driverless vehicles, and remote surgery to become more practical. The delay that occurs between a user's request and the cloud's answer is nearly removed thanks to the low latency that 5G provides. This results in a significantly improved user experience.

Edge computing is the processing of data at a location that is closer to the user or source of the data. 5G technology makes edge computing possible. This indicates that data is not necessary sent back to a centralized data center but rather is handled locally or in close proximity to the point of origin. Edge computing can cut down on latency, speed up reaction times, and save bandwidth all at the same time. Processing of data can take place in real time, making it possible for cloud apps to produce results instantly.

Network Slicing: The network slicing feature of 5G is a useful addition to cloud computing since it enables network operators to dynamically assign resources and tailor those resources to the requirements of a variety of applications. This ensures that cloud apps will have the highest potential level of performance because they will be able to receive the network resources they require in real time.

The Role of Cloud Computing in Making 5G Possible

Cloud computing offers the scalability and flexibility required to facilitate the quick deployment and scaling of 5G networks. Cloud computing also provides the necessary infrastructure and resources. On-demand provisioning and de-provisioning of cloud resources fully aligns with the dynamic requirements of 5G networks. Cloud resources can also be used interchangeably. This scalability means that 5G networks are capable of efficiently adapting to varying demands, whether those demands are caused by large-scale events or by everyday swings in network usage.

Efficiency in Allocation and Utilization of Network Resources Cloud-based network functions, such as Network Function Virtualization (NFV) and Software-Defined Networking (SDN), make it possible to allocate and utilize network resources in an efficient manner. This leads to cost reductions as well as improvements in the performance of the network. The ability of network operators to optimize their resources in response to real-time demands results in a network that is both more efficient and more responsive.

Cloud computing enables automation and orchestration of network functions in 5G networks. These capabilities are referred to as "Orchestration and Automation."

Orchestration technologies allow operators to manage and deliver network services more effectively, which is a significant benefit. Automation helps to streamline network operations, lowering the number of manual processes and the number of errors caused by humans. This ends up producing a 5G network that is more responsive, agile, and efficient with its resources.

The Effects on a Number of Different Sectors

The fact that cloud computing and 5G networking are complementary technologies has significant repercussions for a wide range of businesses and industries.

Telecommunications: Companies that work in telecommunications stand to gain from improved network capabilities and the more effective allocation of resources. They are able to provide their consumers with a more extensive selection of services and applications, which opens the door to new revenue streams. In addition, the implementation of edge computing makes it possible for telecom carriers to deliver low-latency services, which in turn makes real-time apps easier to use.

In the field of healthcare, the combination of 5G wireless technology with cloud computing has the potential to usher in a wave of revolutionary new applications. Real-time monitoring, telesurgery, and other forms of remote medical treatment are all capable of being carried out with high dependability and low latency. This facilitates the transmission of essential medical data in a secure manner and without delay.

Manufacturing: The manufacturing industry stands to benefit from the convergence of these technologies through the adoption of IoT devices connected to 5G networks and data analytics performed in the cloud. By leveraging real-time data from their factories and supply networks, manufacturers may improve product quality, optimize production processes, and reduce the amount of time their production lines are down.

Applications that make use of the Internet of Things (IoT) will benefit tremendously from the combination of 5G and cloud computing. In combination with the processing power of the cloud, the high bandwidth, low latency, and scalable characteristics of 5G networks make it possible to connect and manage an enormous number of Internet of Things devices in an effective manner. This is absolutely necessary for smart cities, smart homes, industrial IoT, and a variety of other applications.

Convergence of 5G wireless networking and cloud computing is an essential component for the research, development, and commercialization of autonomous cars.

Because of the reduced latency of 5G networks, it will be possible for vehicles to communicate with one another and with the infrastructure that supports traffic in real time. Meanwhile, resources hosted in the cloud are able to collect and analyze massive volumes of data generated by sensors and cameras, making it possible for autonomous vehicles to operate in a manner that is both safe and effective.

Concerns and Things to Take Into Account

The complementary nature of the 5G and cloud computing technologies brings with it a number of considerable benefits; nevertheless, it also raises a number of issues that must be addressed.

Safety and Confidentiality: With increased connection and data flow comes an increased need for stringent safety precautions. The protection of sensitive data, the maintenance of users' privacy, and the prevention of attacks via cyberspace are of the utmost importance.

Management of Networks: Managing complicated 5G networks and cloud resources necessitates the use of cutting-edge tools and a high level of skill. In order to assure optimal performance, network operators need to make investments in knowledgeable staff as well as sophisticated management tools.

Concerns Regarding Regulatory and Compliance Issues The convergence may give rise to concerns regarding regulatory and compliance issues, particularly in sectors such as healthcare and finance. It is absolutely necessary to ensure compliance with all data protection legislation, standards, and government policies.

Impact on the Environment The proliferation of 5G networks and cloud computing both have implications for the environment, including the consumption of more energy and the generation of more electronic waste. It is critical to engage in activities that are helpful to the environment.

A new era of creativity, connectivity, and computing is being ushered in as a result of the complementary nature of 5G and cloud technologies. The way we live, work, and interact with the digital world is being fundamentally transformed as a result of their combined efforts. It is essential to solve obstacles such as security, network management, and regulatory issues in order to enable a smooth and secure transition into this disruptive era. Although the benefits are enormous, resolving these challenges is critical. The convergence of 5G and cloud technologies presents the promise of a brighter and more connected future, one in which the possibilities are limited only by our imagination and inventiveness as a species.

3.2 Scalability and flexibility with cloud-driven 5G networks

The landscape of connectivity and communication is undergoing a transformation as a result of the confluence of cloud computing and 5G technology. This convergence provides network operators and enterprises with new levels of scalability and flexibility, making it one of the most enticing parts of the phenomenon. In this piece, we will look into the potentially game-changing capabilities of cloud-driven 5G networks, with a particular emphasis on their scalability and flexibility.

Comprehending the Concept of Cloud-Driven 5G Networks

It is vital to have a firm grasp of the fundamental ideas that support this convergence before delving into the scalability and flexibility of cloud-driven 5G networks.

An Overview of the 5G Technology

Enhanced Data Transfer Speeds When compared to 4G networks, data transfer speeds on 5G networks are significantly faster. Users can enjoy data rates that are greater than 1 Gbps, which makes it possible for them to quickly download and upload data.

Reduced Latencies: One of the goals of 5G is to reduce latencies to one millisecond or less. This would make it perfect for applications that require real-time reactions, such as augmented reality (AR), virtual reality (VR), driverless vehicles, and remote surgery.

Slicing the Network: 5G networks are designed with the flexibility to generate virtual networks that are tailored for certain use cases. This makes it possible to efficiently allocate resources to a variety of applications.

Computing in the Cloud Amid 5G Networks

The computing done in the cloud serves as the framework for cloud-driven 5G networks. Cloud computing offers network operators a scalable and flexible set of resources that are capable of being dynamically allocated to suit the ever-evolving requirements of 5G networks. The following are important ideas related to cloud computing:

On-Demand Service: Because cloud resources are made accessible on-demand, network operators have the ability to provision and de-provision services and infrastructure according to their specific requirements. This is a wonderful fit for the dynamic requirements that 5G networks demand.

Pooling of Resources: Cloud service providers are able to pool and share their resources with various customers, which results in more effective usage of those resources and cost savings. The quick distribution of resources to areas with the greatest need is made possible as a result of this pooling of resources.

Scalability refers to the ability of cloud resources to swiftly increase or decrease in size, which enables network operators to adapt their services to changing levels of network demand. The capacity of 5G networks to satisfy the requirements of large-scale events or abrupt spikes in consumption can be ensured by their ability to scale resources according to those needs.

Scalability in 5G Networks that Are Driven by the Cloud

Cloud-based 5G networks enable resource elasticity, which is also known as elastic cloud computing. In order for network operators to fulfill the demands of high-traffic events like concerts, sporting contests, or emergency circumstances, they are able to swiftly deploy additional processing, storage, or networking resources. This elasticity guarantees that the network will continue to be responsive and will be able to handle workloads of various intensities.

Slicing of the Network: The capability of slicing the network that 5G provides is a potent instrument for scalability. It provides operators with the ability to generate virtual network segments that can be tailored to the requirements of a variety of applications. This means that important applications, such as remote surgery or autonomous vehicles, can receive specialized resources when they are required, which ensures that their performance will be at its highest possible level.

Edge computing is made possible by the confluence of 5G and cloud technologies, which also makes edge computing possible. Computing at the edge enables data to be processed closer to its point of origin, hence minimizing the need for data to travel to and from centralized data centers. This reduces the amount of latency that occurs and provides faster response times, both of which are necessary characteristics for real-time applications. The scalability demanded by applications for immediate access to cloud resources can be met by edge computing, which provides this capability.

Scalability at a Lower Total Cost Cloud-based 5G networks enable scalability at a lower total cost. By dynamically allocating resources in accordance with real-time requests, network operators can prevent themselves from over-provisioning. This effective utilization of resources results in financial savings as well as a more environmentally friendly infrastructure for the network.

Cloud-based flexibility in fifth-generation wireless networks

Dynamic Resource Allocation: The cloud-driven nature of 5G networks makes it possible for network operators to dynamically assign resources. Operators are able to maximize resource utilization for a variety of applications and services when they have the flexibility to dynamically supply and de-provision resources as needed.

The flexibility of the cloud enables network operators to rapidly deploy new services and applications. This is made possible by the rapid deployment of new services. The agility of the cloud enables a rapid deployment of services, which can be used for a variety of purposes, including the introduction of cutting-edge features, the establishment of new network services, and the fulfillment of ever-evolving client requirements.

Cloud-based management solutions provide network operators with the freedom to administer their networks remotely, allowing them to take advantage of remote management and automation. This is especially important for troubleshooting problems remotely, making changes to configurations, and updating software. Automation improves flexibility even further by cutting down on the number of manual operations and errors caused by humans.

Application Development and Innovation: Cloud-driven 5G networks give developers the ability to more simply construct and deploy applications. They don't have to worry about managing complicated infrastructure because they can utilize cloud resources and development tools to come up with fresh ideas and construct new applications. This adaptability is absolutely necessary in order to maintain a competitive edge in a technological landscape that is always shifting.

Concerns and Things to Take Into Account

Security and Privacy: The increased connection and data flow necessitate robust security measures to protect sensitive data and ensure privacy. These steps are necessary in order to ensure that privacy is maintained. This is especially important for applications in the healthcare industry, the financial sector, and other industries with rigorous standards for data protection.

Management of Networks: Managing complicated 5G networks and cloud resources necessitates the use of cutting-edge tools and the expertise of trained professionals. In order to guarantee the best possible performance from their networks, owners and operators of those networks have to put money into the education of their employees and the creation of complex management systems.

Concerns Regarding Regulation and Compliance The convergence of 5G and cloud technologies may give rise to concerns regarding regulation and compliance, particularly in industries that have very stringent regulatory frameworks. It is absolutely necessary to ensure compliance with all of the data protection requirements, industry standards, and government policies.

Impact on the Environment The proliferation of 5G networks and cloud computing both have implications for the environment, including the consumption of more energy and the generation of more electronic waste. It is vital to implement methods that are friendly to the environment in order to reduce the influence on the environment.

A new era of connectivity is being driven by the combination of cloud computing with 5G technology, which offers levels of scalability and flexibility that have never been seen before. Because of this convergence, network operators now have the ability to effectively allocate resources, swiftly launch services, and satisfy the dynamic demands of a digital landscape that is continually expanding. Despite the fact that there are obstacles and things to think about, the revolutionary potential of cloud-driven 5G networks promises a future in which connectivity and innovation can reach unprecedented heights. The prospects for enterprises, industries, and society in general are increasing significantly as this convergence continues to advance. There are no limits to these opportunities.

3.3 Challenges in integrating 5G and cloud

The combination of fifth-generation (5G) wireless networking with cloud computing is a potent synergy that holds the potential to usher in a new era of connection and computing. However, just like the incorporation of any disruptive technology, this one comes with its fair share of difficulties. Network operators, enterprises, and other technology players need to address a variety of difficulties to ensure a smooth and effective integration as these two technologies continue to converge. In this post, we will discuss some of the primary obstacles that must be overcome in order to integrate 5G with the cloud.

1. Concerns Regarding Safety

   When it comes to the integration of 5G and cloud technologies, security is of the utmost importance. This convergence has led to an increase in both the connectivity of devices and the flow of data, both of which present new opportunities for cybercriminals to launch attacks. It is of the utmost importance to protect users' privacy and keep their data secure, particularly in applications relating to healthcare, the financial sector, and essential infrastructure.

Integration of security presents a number of challenges, including:

Protecting the network infrastructure against cyber threats, such as Distributed Denial of Service (DDoS) assaults and attempts to break in, is a major priority when it comes to network security. In order to protect the network from vulnerabilities such as these, operators of the network must implement stringent security measures.

Encryption of Data: Data must be encrypted both while in transit and while it is stored in order to prevent unauthorized access. This is of utmost significance in applications that deal with sensitive information, such as telemedicine, in which patient information must be kept confidential.

Compliance is a big challenge because it involves meeting governmental regulations as well as industry standards for the protection of data and privacy. Compliance with rules such as the HIPAA (Health Insurance Portability and Accountability Act) and the GDPR (General Data Protection Regulation) demands careful attention.

Establishing secure identity and access management (IAM) practices is an absolutely essential step. It is the responsibility of the operators of the network and the suppliers of cloud services to ensure that only authorized personnel can access and alter the resources and data.

2. Management and Orchestration of Network Resources

The difficulty of managing integrated 5G and cloud networks, due to their complexity, presents a considerable problem. Operators of networks are required to traverse a complex environment consisting of virtualized network services, computers at the network's edge, and dynamic resource allocation in the cloud.

The following are examples of challenges faced in network management and orchestration:

Automation: Tools for sophisticated orchestration and automation are necessary for successfully managing these complex networks. Automating tasks like scaling, configuring networks, and allocating resources helps reduce the likelihood of mistakes being made by humans.

Integration of Legacy Systems Many network operators already have legacy systems and infrastructure in place, which must be integrated. It may be difficult to integrate these systems with cloud technologies and 5G networks. There is a possibility that compatibility issues will occur, and in order to prevent disruptions in service, smooth integration is required.

Slicing the Network While network slicing does give flexibility, it also adds complexity to the management of the underlying network. A high level of skill is required in order to correctly configure and manage network slices in order to fulfill the diverse requirements of different applications.

3. Obstacles Presented by Regulations and Compliance

    The integration of 5G and cloud technologies may present difficulties with regard to regulatory frameworks and compliance requirements, in particular in industries that already have stringent regulatory frameworks, such as the healthcare and financial industries. Important factors to take into consideration include conformity with relevant data protection rules, industry standards, and government policies.

    Integration of regulatory and compliance requirements presents a number of challenges, including:

    Data Residency: Different nations have different policies surrounding data residency, which can effect the storage and processing of data in the cloud. These regulations can also vary from country to country. The operators of a network are responsible for ensuring that they comply with all applicable regional, national, and international data residency rules.

    Regarding the protection of user information, the processing of personal data is subject to very specific restrictions. Data protection and stringent privacy policies are something that cloud service providers and operators of public networks are required to put in place.

    Compliance on the Part of Vendors It is of the utmost importance to guarantee that cloud service providers and vendors of network equipment comply with all applicable legislation and standards. In order to ensure compliance, network operators need to thoroughly investigate their technological partners.

4. Considerations Regarding the Environment

    The proliferation of 5G and cloud technology has potential adverse effects on the environment. Both data centers and network infrastructure use a substantial amount of energy, and the disposal of electronic trash can have adverse effects on the environment. It is imperative to put eco-friendly strategies into action if one wishes to reduce the negative impact that this convergence will have on the environment.

The following are examples of environmental integration challenges:

Efficiency in Energy Use Data centers and the equipment used in networks can be quite energy-intensive. The reduction of the carbon footprint caused by these technologies presents a problem, as it requires the use of energy-efficient technologies, renewable energy sources, and efficient cooling systems.

Waste Electronics Getting rid of old network equipment and other electronic waste can be difficult. It is essential to ensure responsible disposal techniques and recycling procedures in order to lessen the impact on the environment.

Green Computing: One of the most major challenges in lowering the amount of energy that is used by data centers is encouraging the adoption of green computing methods. These activities include virtualizing servers and using hardware that is efficient with energy.

5. Compatibility and Adherence to Standards

When it comes to ensuring that the integration of 5G and cloud technologies goes off without a hitch, interoperability and strict adherence to standards are very necessary. It's possible that different manufacturers will have their own proprietary solutions, which may lead to compatibility problems and disrupt the normally smooth operation of these technologies.

Interoperability and standards integration present a number of challenges, including the following:

Lock-In of Vendors: Some network operators and enterprises may find themselves unable to migrate to new solutions or adopt new technologies because they have become locked into specific vendors or technologies. Open standards and actions to promote interoperability are absolutely necessary for preventing vendor lock-in.

The quick pace of technology advancement may be able to outpace the establishment of industry standards as they are developed. Network operators and cloud service providers have a responsibility to be educated and actively participate in groups that establish standards in order to guarantee compatibility and consistency.

6. Capabilities and Areas of Expertise

In order to successfully integrate 5G and cloud technology, professional staff with knowledge in both of these areas is required. It is a big obstacle that there is a shortage of competent experts that are able to manage and run these sophisticated systems.

Integration of talents and expertise presents a number of challenges, including:

Education and Training: In order to ensure that their employees have the knowledge and expertise required to manage and maintain cloud-based 5G networks, network operators need to invest in the education and training of their employees.

A Highly Competitive Job Market Can Be Difficult to Attract and Keep Talent It can be difficult to attract and keep qualified individuals in a highly competitive job market. In order to attract and keep the best employees, network operators need to provide competitive compensation and benefits.

7. Expenses and Return on Investment

The integration of 5G and cloud technologies requires considerable initial investments as well as continuing financial commitments. In order to ensure the smooth integration of these technologies, network operators and organizations must carefully manage their financial resources and establish a hierarchy for their investments.

Integration of costs and investments presents a number of challenges, including the following:

Capital Expenditure: The initial costs of constructing 5G infrastructure, modernizing data centers, and acquiring cloud services can be large. These three projects fall under the category of "capital expenditures." The operators of networks and businesses alike are responsible for practicing efficient capital expenditure management.

Expenses Related to Operations: Ongoing expenses related to operations, such as network maintenance, subscriptions to cloud services, and energy prices, can put a strain on budgets. It is necessary to handle costs in an efficient manner.

The combination of 5G wireless networking and cloud computing technologies holds enormous promise for a future that is more connected, efficient, and innovative. However, these advances in technology come with a series of issues that need to be addressed by network operators, businesses, and other technology stakeholders. The most important things to do are things like addressing concerns about security, managing complicated network settings, maintaining regulatory compliance, and lowering environmental effect.

In addition, a successful integration requires a requirement for interoperability as well as adherence to standards, the acquisition of the required skills and experience, and the efficient management of expenses and investments.

The convergence of 5G and cloud technologies is poised to alter industries and improve the way in which people connect with one another, interact with one another, and innovate in the digital age after these difficulties have been overcome.

3.4 Real-world examples of 5G and cloud convergence

Convergence of 5G and cloud technologies is altering the way organizations function and causing widespread disruption across multiple industries. Because of this synergy, numerous solutions and applications have been developed that make use of the strength of high-speed, low-latency connectivity paired with the scalability and flexibility of cloud computing. In this article, we will examine real-world instances of how the confluence of 5G and the cloud is making a practical influence across a variety of industries. Specifically, we will look at how the healthcare industry is being impacted.

1. **Intelligent Production Systems**

    The manufacturing industry is undergoing a paradigm shift due to the convergence of 5G and cloud technologies, which has led to the development of the idea of "smart factories." In order to connect machinery, sensors, and production systems, manufacturers are taking advantage of the high-speed and low-latency capabilities of 5G networks. This makes it possible for manufacturers to transmit and analyze data in real time. Cloud computing is used to interpret and store the huge volumes of data that are generated. This provides insights that may be utilized for predictive maintenance, quality control, and management of supply chains. This integration results in higher productivity as well as cost savings as a result of the streamlining of production processes, the reduction of downtime, and the optimization of resource allocation.

2. **Remote medical treatment and the use of telemedicine**

    The healthcare sector has benefited significantly from the confluence of 5G and cloud technology, which has led to considerable breakthroughs. Healthcare professionals are able to deliver real-time telemedicine services, conduct remote consultations, and perform complex surgeries with the support of augmented reality (AR) and virtual reality (VR) instruments thanks to the ultra-low latency and high bandwidth of 5G networks. Cloud computing makes it possible to store and analyze patient data in a secure manner, giving medical personnel access to patients' complete medical histories and enabling them to provide individualized care regardless of geographic limits. Because of this convergence, patient outcomes are getting better, accessibility to healthcare services is getting better, and the strain on traditional healthcare facilities is getting less.

3. **Self-Driving Cars and Trucks**

   The research and implementation of autonomous vehicles is being propelled forward by the convergence of 5G and cloud computing technologies. Real-time data transmission between vehicles and their surroundings requires low-latency and high-bandwidth connection, both of which are provided by 5G networks. Cloud computing enables better navigation, collision avoidance, and predictive maintenance by supporting the processing and analysis of huge volumes of data from car sensors and cameras. This confluence is enhancing road safety and bringing about a revolution in the transportation business. It is also preparing the path for the eventual realization of totally autonomous driving.

4. **Applications for Augmented and Virtual Reality (AR) and Virtual Reality (VR)**

   The confluence of 5G and cloud technologies is boosting the capabilities of augmented reality (AR) and virtual reality (VR) applications, which is altering industries including gaming, entertainment, and education. Users will be able to enjoy fully immersive and interactive virtual environments in real time thanks to the high speed and low latency connectivity offered by 5G networks. There will be no noticeable delays or lag. The processing and display of complicated visuals and simulations is made possible by cloud computing, which enables users to have AR and VR experiences that are both seamless and of a high quality. This integration is fostering innovation in the video gaming industry, making it possible to host virtual concerts and events, and altering education and training by creating immersive learning environments.

5. **Applications of the Internet of Things (IoT)**

   The rapid development and implementation of Internet of Things solutions across a wide range of industries is being fueled by the converging technologies of 5G and the cloud. 5G networks offer the connection and capacity necessary to link a wide variety of Internet of Things devices, making it possible for devices and cloud platforms to communicate and share data in real time. The Internet of Things (IoT) can be used to collect data, which can then be stored, processed, and analyzed using cloud computing. This provides businesses with the ability to get useful insights for predictive maintenance, asset tracking, and supply chain management. This integration is supporting the widespread adoption of linked city solutions, industrial Internet of Things applications, and smart home gadgets, which will ultimately lead to improvements in efficiency, sustainability, and connectivity.

6. Applications for Edge Computing Systems

   The convergence of 5G and cloud technologies has been a driving force behind the rise in popularity of edge computing solutions. It will be possible to undertake data processing and analysis closer to the source, thanks to the high-speed and low-latency capabilities of 5G networks. This will cut down on the amount of data that needs to be sent to and from centralized data centers. The implementation of edge computing infrastructure and services can be facilitated by cloud computing, which in turn enables real-time data processing for applications such as video analytics, industrial automation, and Internet of Things devices.

   This convergence is increasing the efficacy of data processing, decreasing the amount of congestion in networks, and making it possible for the rapid deployment of edge computing solutions across a variety of business sectors.

7. Improvements Made to Shopping Experiences

The retail sector is undergoing a transformation as a result of the confluence of 5G and cloud technologies, which is improving the customer experience and enabling personalized offerings. Retailers will be able to provide customers with immersive in-store experiences, interactive product demos, and real-time inventory management thanks to the seamless and high-speed connectivity provided by 5G networks. Cloud computing enables the storing and analysis of client data, which in turn makes it easier to provide tailored suggestions, conduct marketing campaigns that are specifically targeted, and manage supply chains in an effective manner. This connection is boosting customer involvement while also pushing digital transformation inside the industry, which is transforming the landscape of retail in the process.

Chapter 4

Transforming Network Infrastructure

The infrastructure of networks all across the world is undergoing a significant upheaval at the moment. The progression of technology, shifting preferences among users, and an ever-expanding digital ecosystem are the primary impetuses behind this transformation. The infrastructure of networks, which was traditionally distinguished by rigid and static systems, is currently undergoing a profound transition toward flexibility, scalability, and agility. During this in-depth investigation, we will look into the transformative journey of network infrastructure, including its impact on many industries and society as a whole, as well as the key drivers of change.

1. The Opening Statements
   Since the beginning of the internet, there has been significant development in network infrastructure, which serves as the foundation of worldwide communication and the transport of data. The landscape of connectivity is undergoing a transformation as a result of the digital revolution, which is being fuelled by the exponential growth of data, the advent of new technologies, and the evolving expectations of users. This transition is not merely an improvement; rather, it represents a significant shift in the ways in which we connect with one another, communicate with one another, and work together.
2. The Forces That Are Driving the Change
1. The Growth of Data on an Exponential Scale
   A staggering amount of information is being produced and transported throughout the world at an ever-increasing rate. The proliferation of linked devices, the advent of the Internet of Things (IoT), the acceptance of high-definition content, and the increasing

digitization of sectors are some of the causes that are driving this boom. Other factors include the adoption of high-definition content.

2. Computing in the Cloud

    The cloud has emerged as the primary support system for today's network infrastructure. Computing in the cloud provides a level of adaptability, scalability, and cost-effectiveness that is unrivaled by on-premises solutions in their traditional forms. This transition has caused the role of the network to be rethought as a result of the fact that organizations now store data, do computations, and run applications in the cloud.

3. Mobility and the Technology of the 5G Generation

    Connectivity is undergoing a sea change as a result of developments like the implementation of 5G networks and the proliferation of mobile devices. Real-time applications and the expansion of the Internet of Things (IoT) can both benefit from the incredible speed, decreased latency, and network slicing capabilities offered by 5G.

4. IoT (Internet of Things)

    The Internet of Things has resulted in the proliferation of a wide variety of connected gadgets, ranging from intelligent home appliances to sensors used in industrial settings. These devices need to be connected to a network in order to share data and permit remote control, which raises new concerns regarding scalability and dependability.

5. Computing on the Edge

    Computing at the edge brings data processing closer to the point of origin, which decreases latency and enables the development of real-time applications. It has risen to prominence in a number of industries, including remote healthcare delivery, industrial automation, and autonomous cars.

6. A.I. and ML (Machine Learning and Artificial Intelligence)

The use of artificial intelligence (AI) and machine learning helps improve network security, optimize network administration, and forecast the need for network repair. The implementation of these technologies gives network operations more intelligence, which in turn makes those operations more efficient and responsive.

III. The Evolving Nature of the Network Infrastructure

The transformation of network infrastructure involves a variety of different aspects, each of which contributes to an environment that is a network that is more agile, efficient, and adaptive.

1. Software-Defined Networking (SDN)
   The software-defined network (SDN) is an essential enabler of the revolution. This allows for centralized network management as well as dynamic setup by decoupling the control plane from the data plane. The flexibility of the network is increased by SDN, which enables administrators to respond more swiftly to changing requirements.
2. The acronym NFV stands for "network function virtualization."
   Network functions that have historically required specialized hardware, such as firewalls and load balancers, can be virtualized with the help of NFV. The management of the network is made more easier, costs are cut down, and the deployment of services is sped up because to this flexibility.
3. Computing on the Edge
   Computing at the edge brings data processing closer to the point of origin, which decreases latency and enables the development of real-time applications. It is a game-changer for applications that require fast reactions, such as industrial automation and driverless vehicles.
4. Multi-Access Edge Computing (often referred to as MEC)
   The capabilities of edge computing are brought closer to the mobile network's periphery via MEC. It gives programs the ability to have extremely low latency and a high bandwidth, which is what makes real-time experiences possible.
5. Networks for 5G
   5G is at the forefront of the evolution of network technology. It provides exceptionally fast data transfer rates, decreased lag time, and the ability to slice networks. The inclusion of these elements paves the way for the development of cutting-edge applications such as remote surgery, augmented reality (AR), and the Internet of Things (IoT).
6. Architectures that are Native to the Cloud
   As a result of the shift toward cloud-native architectures, apps are now being developed with cloud environments in mind from the beginning. This method is essential to the DevOps philosophy as it helps to streamline the development and deployment processes.
7. The Automation and Orchestration of the Network

Tools for automation and orchestration cut down on the need for manual network management, hence reducing the likelihood of errors caused by humans and boosting productivity. These tools are absolutely necessary for managing environments of complicated and ever-changing networks.

IV. The Influence on the Various Industries

The development of network infrastructure is having a dramatic impact on a variety of sectors, ushering in new possibilities and altering processes that have been around for a long time.

1. Health care services

   Telemedicine, remote surgery, and real-time monitoring are all made possible thanks to advancements in network infrastructure that have been made in the medical field. Patients are able to obtain medical treatments without having to leave the convenience of their own homes, and healthcare practitioners are able to give care that is both fast and effective.

2. Industrial Production

   The deployment of smart factories provides advantages to the manufacturing industry as a result of network transformation. The use of real-time data analytics, remote equipment monitoring, and predictive maintenance all contribute to an improvement in product quality, as well as a reduction in the amount of downtime experienced.

3. Commerce in stores

   In the retail industry, network transformation results in improved experiences for the end user (the customer). Retailers can improve inventory management, provide more personalized product recommendations, and create more immersive in-store experiences by utilizing real-time data analytics.

4. A formal education

   The rise of online learning platforms and virtual classrooms has brought about a sea change in the educational system, which has been brought about by the transformation brought about by the internet. Both students and professors are able to join from any location, and educational institutions are able to communicate with people all over the world.

5. Travel and communication

   The arrival of autonomous vehicles, which will be made possible by 5G and edge computing, is about to usher in a new era in the transportation industry. It is anticipated that these cars will transform the logistics business, in addition to improving road safety and reducing congestion.

6. Amusements and diversions

Streaming in high definition, immersive gaming experiences, and virtual concerts and events are some examples of the ways that the entertainment business might benefit from the evolution of network infrastructure. The delivery of content is smooth, which enhances the overall user experience.

V. Obstacles and Things to Take Into Account

1. Safekeeping
   Network security is of the utmost importance in this day and age of increased connection and data flow. The protection of sensitive data, the maintenance of users' privacy, and the prevention of attacks via cyberspace are all absolutely necessary.
2. Management of the Network
   The management of dynamic and complicated networks calls for sophisticated technologies and extensive experience. In order to assure optimal performance, network operators need to make investments in knowledgeable staff as well as sophisticated management tools.
3. Concerns Relating to Regulations and Compliance
   The modernization of network infrastructure may present difficulties in achieving regulatory and compliance standards, in particular in sectors such as the healthcare and financial industries. It is absolutely necessary to ensure compliance with all data protection legislation, standards, and government policies.
4. The Influence on the Environment

The expansion of network infrastructure brings with it a number of environmental concerns, including the consumption of more energy and the accumulation of more electronic waste. It is vital to implement methods that are friendly to the environment in order to reduce the influence on the environment.

As a result of the development of network architecture, the rules governing connectivity and communication are being rewritten. It is altering how we live and work in the digital age, as well as the industries that it is boosting, and it is fueling innovation. The opportunities for companies, industries, and society in general are expanding exponentially as network infrastructure continues to undergo continuous development. Taking on difficulties, being open to innovation, and being able to adjust to the ever-changing world of network connectivity are essential steps in achieving a successful transformation.

4.1 Virtualization of network functions (NFV)

The virtualization of network functions, also known as Network Function Virtualization (NFV) in common parlance, has emerged as a potent force capable of bringing about fundamental change in the field of networking. NFV enables flexibility, scalability, and cost-efficiency in network design, management, and operation by detaching network functions from specialized hardware and implementing them as software-based solutions. This is redefining how networks are designed, managed, and operated. In this piece, we will investigate the idea of NFV, as well as its significance, potential applications in the real world, and the future that it offers.

1. Acquiring a Solid Foundational Knowledge of Network Function Virtualization (NFV)

   Network Function Virtualization (NFV) is an innovative strategy for planning, delivering, and managing network services. At its foundation, NFV is an acronym that stands for "network function virtualization." It entails converting historically hardware-bound network operations into software-based applications that are capable of running on common servers, storage, and switches that can be purchased from any retailer. This shift in perspective makes it possible to decouple the functions of the network from the underlying hardware, which ultimately results in network services that are more flexible, scalable, and cost-effective.
2. The Most Important Aspects of NFV
1. Adaptability and quickness of movement

   Flexibility is one of the fundamental principles that underpins NFV. Organizations are able to swiftly adapt to changing network demands, add or remove services as needed, and respond to new requirements when network functions are virtualized. This eliminates the need for extensive hardware changes. This adaptability is absolutely necessary in the ever-changing digital landscape.
2. Capacity to Grow

   Network functions that are virtualized have the ability to scale up or down depending on what is required, which allows them to accommodate variations in network traffic, application demand, or user activity. The ability to scale up or down guarantees that network resources are used effectively and that services can adapt to changing levels of user demand.
3. An Economy of Expenditure

   Because to NFV, there is less of a need for dedicated and specialized hardware, which results in significant cost reductions. Commercially available off-the-shelf (COTS) hardware can be utilized by

businesses, and resources can be allocated according to operational requirements. This can result in more cost-effective network infrastructure.
4. Immediate Deployment of Services

The implementation of network services and functionalities can proceed much more quickly thanks to NFV. Because software rather than labor-intensive hardware installations are used to implement new services and updates, rollout times for these features can be reduced significantly. In today's lightning-fast technological climate, the ability to rapidly deploy solutions is a significant competitive advantage.

III. Practical Applications of NFV in the Real World

1. Wireless and wired communications
    NFV is being utilized by providers of telecommunications services in order to improve the effectiveness and scalability of their networks. Firewalls, load balancers, and network address translation are examples of the kinds of services that are included in virtualized network functions. Telcos are able to improve their infrastructure, lower their expenses, and swiftly deploy new services when they make the switch from dedicated appliances to functions that are virtualized.
2. Computing at the Edge
    Edge computing would not be possible without the crucial part played by NFV. Organizations are able to increase the performance of real-time applications and lower their overall latency levels by putting virtualized network operations at the edge of the network, which is physically located closer to the data source. Edge computing can be used in a variety of contexts, including augmented reality, driverless cars, and industrial automation.
3. Companies that offer services in the cloud
    NFV is used by cloud service providers to improve the efficiency of their data centers and the quality of the services they supply. The virtualization of network functions enables service providers to provide their consumers scalable and configurable network services. Examples of virtualized network functions include virtual routers and virtual private networks (VPNs).
4. Business and Corporate Networking
    NFV is becoming increasingly popular among businesses as a means to simplify their networking infrastructure. Virtualized network functions offer a solution that is both nimble and economical for

services such as software-defined wide-area networking (SD-WAN), network security, and virtual private clouds (VPCs). Taking this method streamlines network management and lessens the burden of operational responsibilities.

5. IoT (Internet of Things)

When it comes to meeting the connection and data processing requirements of the Internet of Things (IoT), NFV is an absolute necessity. Applications that make use of the Internet of Things frequently need for scalable and effective network services such data filtering, routing, and analysis. IoT data may be processed and sent more efficiently thanks to virtualized network services, which guarantee this.

IV. Obstacles and Factors to Consider When Implementing NFV

NFV, although its many advantages, also poses a number of difficulties and requires careful attention.

1. Protection of Computer Networks

   The migration to virtualized network functions necessitates the implementation of stringent security protocols. As more and more network tasks are moved into software, the risks associated with those functions increase. It is vital to put into place security solutions that secure virtualized functions and monitor network traffic.

2. Capacity for cooperation

   It can be difficult to ensure that multiple virtualized network functions from different vendors can work together without any interruptions. In order to avoid compatibility concerns, standardized interfaces and interoperability testing are absolutely necessary.

3. The Distribution of Resources

   It is absolutely necessary to allot resources to virtualized network tasks in an appropriate manner in order to keep performance and scalability intact. The utilization of organizational resources must be monitored, and the organization's functions must be provided with the resources they require.

4. Skill Acquisition and Experience

A different set of skills is required in order to successfully adopt and manage NFV. Organizations either need to make investments in the training of their information technology personnel or seek out professionals that are knowledgeable in network function management and virtualization.

V. The Prospects for NFV in the Future

1. Implementation of 5G
   When it comes to enabling services and applications that run on 5G networks, network function virtualization (NFV) will be an extremely important factor. The flexibility and scalability needed to support the low latency and high bandwidth of 5G can be provided through network function virtualization (NFV).
2. Developments in Computing at the Edge
   In the context of edge computing, NFV will continue to develop in the coming years. The performance of applications such as autonomous vehicles and remote healthcare will be improved because to NFV's ability to provide real-time data processing and analysis at the edge, which will become more widespread as edge computing gains popularity.
3. Methods of Automated Control and Orchestration
   The level of sophistication of the technologies used for automation and orchestration will increase, which will make the deployment and maintenance of virtualized network operations easier. The use of AI and machine learning will lead to additional improvements in the optimization and security of networks.
4. Incorporation of Cloud-Native Architectural Frameworks
   NFV will be compatible with cloud-native designs, which will make it possible to create network functions that are tailored exclusively for use in cloud settings. The development process will be simplified as a result, and the scalability of network services will be improved.
5. Additional Safety and Protective Measures

The security facet of NFV will continue to develop, with the primary emphasis being placed on the implementation of innovative security solutions that shield virtualized functions from potential cyberattacks.

The implementation of network function virtualization, often known as NFV, is a significant paradigm shift in the manner in which networks are planned, managed, and operated. Its use is increasing across a wide range of industries and use cases as a direct result of its major features, which include flexibility, scalability, cost-efficiency, and rapid implementation. Despite the fact that there are obstacles to overcome, the future of NFV has an incredible amount of promise, particularly in relation to the integration of 5G, edge computing, automation, and increased security. As NFV continues to develop, it will play an increasingly important part in reshaping the landscape of networking and providing support for the requirements of the digital era.

4.2 Software-defined networking (SDN)

In the field of networking, Software-Defined Networking (SDN) stands out as a paradigm shift that revolutionizes the ways in which networks are planned, managed, and operated. This forward-thinking method of networking separates the control plane from the data plane, which enables network administrators to exercise centralized control and management over the resources of the network.

As a result, there is increased adaptability, fluidity, and productivity. In this piece, we will look into the idea of software-defined networking (SDN), as well as its fundamental concepts, practical implementations, and the significant impact it has on today's networking.

1. Acquiring a Basic Knowledge of Software-Defined Networking (SDN)

    Software-Defined Networking, or SDN for short, is an architectural approach to networking that moves network control away from specialized hardware and toward a controller that is implemented in software. In conventional computer networks, network services such as routing and switching are inextricably bound to certain pieces of physical hardware. By abstracting these operations and managing them through software, software-defined networking (SDN) provides network administrators with a centralized and programmable view of the entire network.

2. The Foundational Concepts of the SDN
1. The ability to separate the control plane from the data plane

    Both the control plane, which is in charge of deciding which route data packets should take, and the data plane, which is in charge of actually transmitting the data packets, are intimately integrated within the network devices that make up traditional networks. These two planes are kept distinct within the SDN. The control plane is overseen and managed by a centralized controller, which is responsible for determining how data should be transmitted. On the other hand, the data plane, which is comprised of various network devices, merely carries out the instructions that are issued by the controller.

2. Control Exercised Centrally

    A central controller operates as the brain of a software-defined network (SDN), making choices that affect the entire network based on the current state of the network. This centralization makes network management more easier and paves the way for worldwide optimization of the network.

3. The capacity to program

Software-defined networks (SDNs) allow for the implementation of network functionalities in software. Because the network can be programmed, administrators have the opportunity to define, regulate, and configure the behavior of the network using various software tools. As a consequence of this, networks become more flexible and responsive to the shifting demands placed upon them.

III. SDN Applications in Real-World Contexts

1. Computer Repository Facilities
   Data center networking is being revolutionized by software-defined networking (SDN), which improves resource allocation and optimizes traffic flows. SDN enables the flexibility to allocate and reallocate resources on demand in highly dynamic data center environments, which ultimately results in the delivery of services that are both quicker and more efficient.
2. Wide Area Networks, Abbreviated as WAN
   The application of SDN to wide area networks is becoming increasingly common. With centralized control, wide area networks (WANs) are able to be dynamically optimized to respond to traffic patterns. This ensures that data travels between geographically scattered locations via the channel that is the most time and cost effective. This is of utmost importance when it comes to linking different branch offices and data centers.
3. Virtual Private Networks, most often known as VPNs
   The establishment of software-based virtual private networks is made possible by
   software-defined networking (SDN). These virtual private networks (VPNs) offer secure communication channels that are encrypted both within an organization and between organizations. This helps to keep data private and prevent unauthorized access to it.
4. Protection of Computer Networks
   By enabling dynamic firewall settings and intrusion detection systems, SDN has the potential to significantly improve network security. It is possible to make fast updates to security rules in order to respond to newly discovered risks, which lowers the chance of security breaches and assaults.
5. Computing in the Cloud
   The use of SDN is important to the functioning of cloud data centers. Cloud service providers make use of software-defined networking (SDN) in order to dynamically assign network resources to virtual machines. This helps to ensure that hosted applications make the most efficient use of available resources.

6. IoT (Internet of Things)

The Internet of Things necessitates the development of adaptable and scalable network infrastructures that are in a position to effectively manage the enormous number of connected devices as well as the varied data flows that these devices produce. SDN makes network management easier, which in turn makes it simpler to connect and manage Internet of Things devices.

IV. The Advantages and the Importance of the SDN

1. Adaptability and quickness of movement
   SDN offers a level of agility and network flexibility that has never been seen before. Organizations are able to quickly respond to changing requirements and launch new services when they have programmable network functions because these capabilities eliminate the need for extensive hardware changes.
2. Administration from a Central Location
   The management and optimization of a network are both made easier by centralized control. Administrators have a comprehensive view of the network and are able to make decisions at the global level to optimize the operation of the network.
3. Improved Safety and Assurance
   The programmable and dynamic nature of SDN makes it possible to make immediate adjustments to network security policies, hence enhancing the network's defense against new threats.
4. An Economy of Expenditure
   SDN eliminates the requirement for expensive, specialized hardware by decoupling network functions from their corresponding dedicated hardware devices. The software-defined network (SDN) makes use of commercially available hardware, which results in lower costs and increased resource utilization.
5. Increased Capacity for Scalability
   SDN networks are naturally more scalable since administrators are able to assign resources according to the specific requirements of the network. This scalability is especially beneficial in settings with varying amounts of work to be done and an increasing number of linked devices.
6. Decreased Amount of Downtime

Changes and updates to the network can be implemented with very little interruption of service when using SDN. This improves the overall availability of the network while simultaneously decreasing the number of service outages.

V. Obstacles and Things to Take Into Account

1. **Concerns Regarding Safety**
   The concentration of power over a network can make it more susceptible to intrusions. It is absolutely necessary to take measures to protect not only the SDN controller but also the network as a whole.
2. **Competence and Instruction**
   A new skill set is required in order to successfully implement and manage SDN. To ensure efficient implementation and management, businesses need to make investments in the training of their information technology personnel.
3. **The capacity for cooperation**
   It is a problem to ensure that different SDN solutions from different suppliers can work together without any disruptions. In order to avoid compatibility concerns, standardized interfaces and interoperability testing are absolutely necessary.
4. **Observance of the Requirements**

Regulatory and compliance standards have to be met by SDN solutions in order for them to be implemented, particularly in sectors where data protection and privacy laws are particularly stringent.

VI. The Prospects for the SDN

1. **Improvements Made to Automation**
   The Software-Defined Network (SDN) will see automation play an even more crucial role. The performance of the network will be improved with the help of artificial intelligence and machine learning, and administrative responsibilities will be simplified.
2. **Combination with the 5G network**
   SDN will become increasingly important as the rollout of 5G networks continues since it will be necessary for enabling the rapid deployment of 5G services and optimizing their performance.
3. **Integration of Edge Computing Technologies**
   The Software Defined Network (SDN) will continue to develop in order to support the particular requirements of edge computing. Real-time applications, such as driverless vehicles and augmented reality, will benefit from the improved performance that this integration will bring about.
4. **Solutions for Improved Safety and Protection**

The evolution of security in SDN will continue to take place in response to newly discovered dangers. In order to protect against cyberattacks, more sophisticated security mechanisms will be built into SDN solutions.

Software-Defined Networking, often known as SDN, is currently in the vanguard of the advancement of networking. Its fundamental ideas, which include separating the control plane from the data plane, centralizing management, and providing programmability, have major implications for networking in a variety of fields, and those implications are far-reaching. SDN has become a vital tool in modern networking because of the advantages it offers in terms of agility, centralization, increased security, and cost efficiency.

Despite the fact that there are obstacles and things to think about, the future of SDN holds the potential of even more automation, integration with 5G and edge computing, as well as improved security solutions. As software-defined networking (SDN) continues to develop, it will reshape the landscape of networking, giving enterprises the ability to construct networks that are more responsive, efficient, and adaptive for the digital age.

4.3 Edge computing and its role in 5G and cloud

Edge computing has emerged as a vital component that bridges the gap between these two game-changing technologies in light of recent developments such as the introduction of 5G and the widespread adoption of cloud computing. The digital landscape is in a state of constant evolution. In this article, we will investigate what edge computing is, its significance in the context of 5G and the cloud, real-world applications, and the future that it offers in transforming the way in which we connect, compute, and communicate with one another.

1. Comprehending the Concept of Edge Computing
   Instead of depending on a centralized data center or a server located in the cloud, a distributed computing paradigm known as edge computing processes data at the "edge" of the network, which is the closest point of proximity to the data source. With edge computing, data processing happens on or near the device or sensors that generate the data. This eliminates the need for the data to travel great distances in order to reach a central data center in order to be processed there.
2. Fundamental Ideas and Their Importance Regarding 5G and the Cloud
1. Very Little Delay
   The concept of minimal latency is one of the key drives behind edge computing.

Edge computing shortens the amount of time it takes for data to travel from the source to the processing point and back, which ultimately results in answers that are very close to instantaneous in situations where real-time processing and reaction are essential, such as in autonomous vehicles, telemedicine, and augmented reality applications.

2. Optimization of the Bandwidth

   The use of bandwidth is optimized using edge computing. Only the data that is pertinent or the results that have been aggregated are sent across the network; this helps to alleviate the strain that is placed on the bandwidth by sending enormous volumes of data to a centralized data center or cloud server.

3. Capacity for Growth and Adaptability

   Edge computing makes it possible to scale the computational resources that are located at the edge. It is a solution that offers a great degree of flexibility since organizations can deploy edge servers whenever they deem it necessary, and they can swiftly adapt to changes in demand.

4. Confidentiality of the Data and Its Location

When edge computing is used, the data stays in its original location and is not transferred via the public internet. Because of the consequences this has for data privacy and sovereignty, it is a decision that is recommended for applications that require stringent data localization or compliance with regulations.

III. Applications of Edge Computing in Real-World Contexts

1. Self-Driving Cars and Trucks

   Computing in the vehicle's periphery is essential in the field of autonomous cars. It frees the onboard sensors and artificial intelligence systems from dependence on a remote data center, allowing them to process data and make choices in real time. Processing with a reduced latency like this improves both safety and responsiveness.

2. The use of telemedicine

   The use of edge computing is ushering in a new era in telemedicine. At the point of care, medical devices can process crucial patient data, securely send that data to off-site physicians, and enable those physicians to make fast choices. When dealing with urgent circumstances, this is of the utmost importance.

3. Robotics and Computers in Industry

   Computing at the edge of networks is an essential component of industrial automation because it enables real-time monitoring and management of production processes. This results in less downtime, a greater boost in efficiency, and it makes predictive maintenance easier to perform.

4. IoT (Internet of Things)

   The Internet of Things makes use of edge computing in order to process the data that is created by the numerous linked devices. This distributed processing improves the ability to efficiently handle and respond to data generated by the Internet of Things, which in turn encourages the development of smart cities, smart homes, and industrial applications for the Internet of Things.

5. Virtual Reality (VR) and Augmented Reality (AR) technologies

   Edge computing is beneficial for augmented reality (AR) and virtual reality (VR) applications because it enables the rendering of sophisticated images and simulations at the edge device, which results in a seamless and immersive experience with little latency.

6. Retail trade

Edge computing improves the whole shopping experience for consumers that frequent retail establishments. Real-time analytics and individualized recommendations can be provided to customers in a retail setting, which boosts both consumer engagement and revenue.

IV. The Importance of Computing at the Periphery in 5G

Both edge computing and 5G are on the cusp of making significant changes to the digital landscape, and they are inextricably linked.

1. Extremely Low Latencies in 5G

   For real-time applications such as autonomous vehicles, remote surgery, and immersive augmented reality and virtual reality experiences, the exceptionally low latency offered by 5G networks is necessary. Edge computing is a useful addition to 5G because it moves processing operations closer to the data source, which further decreases latency and enables interactions to take place instantly.

2. Creating Slices of a Network

   The concept of "network slicing," in which a single physical network may be partitioned into many virtual networks that are suited for certain use cases, is one of the innovations that 5G makes possible. Computing at the edge enables the deployment of edge servers for diverse network slices, which optimizes resource allocation and provides bespoke solutions for a variety of applications.

3. Shifting the Load of Data Traffic

Through the use of edge computing, data traffic on crowded 5G networks can be offloaded. Edge servers have the ability to process data locally, and instead of sending every piece of data to the central cloud, they will just communicate relevant findings or aggregated data. This will reduce the amount of congestion on the network.

V. The Importance of Computing at the Periphery in Cloud

1. The Integration of Clouds
   Computing at the edge and in the cloud can collaborate to produce an ecosystem that is uninterrupted. Edge devices have the ability to process data and transfer the results of their work to the cloud, where it can be stored, analyzed, and further processed. This hybrid approach gives businesses the option to take advantage of the scalability and storage capacity offered by the cloud while also making use of the low-latency processing capabilities offered by the edge.
2. A Cloud That Is Distributed
   The idea of a dispersed cloud is starting to take shape, which entails bringing cloud services to the network's periphery. This method combines the benefits of cloud computing, such as scalability and remote management, with the processing capabilities of edge computing, which are distinguished by their low-latency characteristics.
3. Orchestration from the Edge to the Cloud

Platforms that support integration of edge and cloud resources in a seamless manner are known as edge-to-cloud orchestration platforms. These platforms make it possible to centralize the management of cloud resources and edge devices, so guaranteeing that operations are efficient and well-coordinated.

VI. Obstacles and Things to Take Into Account

1. Safekeeping
   When it comes to edge computing, security is of the utmost importance. Edge devices are frequently situated in uncontrolled situations, which leaves them open to the possibility of being physically tampered with. It is imperative that comprehensive measures be taken to protect data privacy and device security.
2. Capacity for Growth and Administration
   It might be challenging to effectively manage a large number of edge devices. In order to keep an edge computing environment scalable and productive, having effective device management solutions and orchestration platforms is important.

3. The consistency of the data
   It can be difficult to guarantee the same level of data consistency and integrity between edge and cloud resources. In order to reduce the risk of having inconsistent data, businesses need to put in place methods for data synchronization and redundancy.
4. Capacity for cooperation

It is important to ensure that edge devices and cloud services provided by a variety of suppliers are compatible with one another. These issues can be overcome through the implementation of standardization and open interfaces.

VII. The Prospects for Computing at the Edge

1. Improvements to the Integration of AI
   In the future, there will be a deeper integration of artificial intelligence into edge computing, which will make it possible for intelligent decisions to be made at the edge. The use of centralized cloud servers will become less necessary as artificial intelligence algorithms become better at processing and interpreting data on their own.
2. The development of 5G
   The importance of computers at the network's edge will increase in tandem with the rollout of 5G networks. Numerous industries are going to undergo significant shifts as a result of the combination of 5G's high bandwidth and low latency with edge computing's local processing capability.
3. Cloud services that are distributed
   The idea of a dispersed cloud, which provides cloud services at the network's periphery, will become increasingly common. The integration of cloud and edge resources will be completely seamless as a result of this.
4. Collaboration from the Edge to the Core

There will be an increase in direct collaboration between edge devices, which will result in the creation of decentralized ecosystems.

The efficiency of applications such as the Internet of Things, driverless vehicles, and smart cities will improve as a result of this peer-to-peer collaboration.

Computing at the network's edge is revolutionizing how we think about data processing and the responsiveness of networks in the digital age. Edge computing is essential to the convergence of 5G and cloud technologies because of its capacity to lessen the occurrence of delay, increase bandwidth utilization, and make real-time applications possible.

Edge computing is expected to continue its rapid development, which will enable a wide range of businesses to develop new, cutting-edge products and services, such as telemedicine and driverless vehicles. However, for the successful implementation of edge computing in a variety of applications, it is needed to address difficulties relating to security, scalability, data consistency, and interoperability. It is anticipated that the future of digital connectivity will be marked by increased levels of efficacy, responsiveness, and transformation as a result of the combination of edge computing, 5G, and cloud technologies.

4.4 Ensuring security in the transformed network

As the infrastructure of the network undergoes a deep revolution brought on by technologies such as 5G, cloud computing, software-defined networking (SDN), and edge computing, ensuring that the network is secure becomes an issue of the utmost importance. Due to the nature of the rapidly changing digital ecosystem, which is both dynamic and widespread, new difficulties have emerged, which call for the development of novel solutions to protect sensitive data, preserve users' privacy, and defend against cyberattacks. In this article, we will investigate the security problems posed by the altered network, as well as the tactics and technologies that are necessary for preserving security in an environment that is undergoing rapid transformation.

1. The Evolving Nature of Computer Network Safety
   1. **An increased surface area for attacks**
      A bigger attack surface is created for hostile actors as a result of increased connectivity and the proliferation of devices, particularly in the Internet of Things (IoT). The greater the number of points of entry into the network, the greater the number of possible vulnerabilities.
   2. **Environments That Are Always Changing**
      Maintaining a constant security posture can be difficult to achieve in modern networks because of the dynamic nature of these networks, in which resources can be scaled up or down according to user needs. Traditional security methods, which were designed to be used in unchanging contexts, are no longer adequate.
   3. **Control That Is Centralized**

In software-defined networking (SDN) and cloud computing environments, centralized control offers efficiencies and agility but also creates a single point of failure. Attacks that target the control plane have the potential to bring down the entire network.

II. Challenges to Network Security in the Transformed Environment

1. Security on the Edge
   The processing of data can be done closer to its original source with edge computing, which is helpful for applications that are sensitive to latency. On the other hand, edge devices are frequently deployed in locations that are not under direct control, which leaves them open to the risk of both physical and digital assaults.
2. Risks Associated with 5G
   Despite the fact that 5G networks offer low latency and tremendous capacity, they also create new issues for data security. The increasing number of devices that are linked to 5G networks, in conjunction with the capabilities of 5G to slice networks dynamically, creates a scenario in which focused attacks have the potential to cause major harm.
3. Security in the Cloud
   Because cloud systems tend to have a concentration of valuable data and resources, they are an attractive target for hackers. Access to cloud resources must be secured by organizations, along with the protection of data privacy and protection against illegal access.
4. Security Measures for Software-Defined Networking (SDN)
   Because SDN centralizes network control, the controller becomes an important and valuable target. It is absolutely necessary to safeguard the control plane and restrict unwanted access to the SDN's underlying infrastructure.
5. Protection of Internet of Things

IoT devices are vulnerable to security flaws due to the fact that they come from a broad variety of vendors and have a diverse set of characteristics. Securing IoT networks entails taking a holistic approach to defend against existing dangers as well as those that are yet to emerge.

III. Protective Measures for the New Network Architecture

1. Model of Security Based on Zero Trust
   The Zero Trust paradigm operates under the presumption that no user, device, or piece of the network should be trusted by default. Access is allowed according to the "need-to-know" principle, and verification takes place continuously. This paradigm performs exceptionally well in contexts that are both dynamic and distributed.

2. The Division of the Network
   The network is broken up into more manageable pieces through a process called network segmentation. By taking this method, the lateral movement of cyber threats can be restricted, and the attack surface can be minimized. In software-defined networking (SDN) environments, the segmentation of a network is extremely flexible and may be altered on the fly.
3. Extraordinary Authentification and Control of Access
   Only authorized users and devices should be able to access network resources, and this can be ensured by the implementation of multi-factor authentication (MFA) and stringent access control regulations. Granular permissions can be enforced with the help of role-based access control, often known as RBAC.
4. Codes and ciphers
   Encrypting data from beginning to finish provides protection against data theft as well as data modification while it is in transit and while it is stored. It is essential for data to be encrypted whenever it is being stored in a cloud environment.
5. Ongoing surveillance and detection of potential dangers
   Systems for security information and event management (SIEM) and intrusion detection and prevention systems (IDPS) work together to provide real-time monitoring and detection of potentially malicious activity. The detection of anomalies helps pinpoint departures from the typical operation of a network.
6. Training in the Awareness of Security Risks

The level of security is only as reliable as its weakest link, which is typically associated with human behavior. Employees and users are more informed about best practices, phishing awareness, and the necessity of robust password management when they participate in regular security awareness training.

IV. Protective Measures for the New Network Architecture

1. Firewalls for the Next Generation
   The capabilities of traditional firewalls are combined with those of more advanced security technologies found in next-generation firewalls. These technologies include intrusion prevention, deep packet inspection, and application control.
2. Orchestration and Automation of Security Measures
   Platforms for security orchestration and automation can help speed

up the process of responding to threats, which in turn enables quicker containment and elimination of dangers.

3. Intelligence on Potential Dangers

   Integrating threat intelligence feeds and services can assist firms in maintaining an up-to-date awareness of the most recent vulnerabilities and dangers. The proactive security actions that are taken can be informed by this knowledge.

4. Security that is Defined by Software

   In the same way that SDN provides flexible network administration, software-defined security systems may alter their security rules and controls to respond to the changing nature of the threats they face.

5. Safety Measures for Containers

   Containerization is frequently used in cloud-native operating environments. It is essential to implement container security solutions in order to shield containerized applications from any potential dangers.

6. Cloud Access Security Brokers, or CASB for short.

The provision of visibility, compliance, and data security for cloud applications is made possible by CASBs, which are an essential component of cloud environments.

V. Compliance with Regulations and the Protection of Personal Information

It is very necessary to ensure complete compliance with all applicable data protection rules, including the General Data Protection Regulation (GDPR) and the Health Insurance Portability and Accountability Act (HIPAA). Because of the potentially severe consequences of failing to comply with these standards, companies absolutely must check that their preventative safety measures are in line with the requirements.

VI. Using Artificial Intelligence and Machine Learning and Their Role in Today's World

Both artificial intelligence (AI) and machine learning (ML) have important functions to perform in the context of protecting networks. These technologies make it possible to detect and respond proactively to potential threats by spotting abnormalities and trends that conventional security procedures might overlook. In addition to this, they can help automate mundane security duties, which frees up security professionals to concentrate on more difficult problems.

VII. The Prospects for Network Security in a Network That Has Been Transformed

1. **Highly Developed Intelligence Regarding Dangers**
   There will be an increase in the level of sophistication of threat intelligence, which will utilize AI and ML to predict and respond to attacks in real time. In order to accomplish this, threat intelligence platforms will need to be integrated with the security measures.
2. **Improved and Enhanced Automation of Security**
   The use of automation in security operations will become more widespread, which will make threat containment and remediation far quicker. The technique of security orchestration will eventually become the norm.
3. **Ongoing surveillance of the security situation**
   Continuous monitoring and threat detection will become more proactive and predictive in nature, and security measures will be able to adapt to newly emerging threats in real time.
4. **Security that is Powered by AI**

With AI-driven security solutions that are able to make autonomous decisions and react to changing threats, artificial intelligence (AI) will play a more major role in the protection of computer networks.

The difficulty of ensuring network security after it has been modified involves a number of different aspects and calls for a solution that is both comprehensive and dynamic. The rapidly changing nature of the digital landscape, which is being driven by developments in areas such as 5G, cloud computing, software-defined networking (SDN), and edge computing, calls for the development of novel security methods and technologies to protect against an ever-expanding variety of threats.

Important security measures include zero trust, network segmentation, sophisticated authentication, encryption, and constant monitoring. Protection relies heavily on several types of security technology, including firewalls of the next generation, security orchestration and automation, and container security.

A safe transformed network also requires compliance with data protection requirements and the incorporation of artificial intelligence and machine learning into its security mechanisms, both of which are essential components.

Network security will continue to adapt and grow more complex as the digital landscape continues to evolve. Advanced threat intelligence, enhanced security automation, and AI-driven security will play an increasingly essential role in the process of safeguarding the integrity and privacy of networks.

Chapter 5

Applications of 5G and Cloud

A world that is becoming more interconnected is about to enter a new era of creativity and efficiency, and it will be ushered in by the convergence of technologies known as 5G and cloud computing. The combination of high-speed, low-latency 5G networks with the limitless processing capacity of the cloud holds the potential to revolutionize entire industries, improve customer experiences, and propel the advancement of technology. In this exhaustive investigation, we will delve into the numerous uses of 5G and cloud computing, covering a wide array of industries and use cases that are destined to alter how we live, work, and connect in the digital era. These applications are expected to have a significant impact on how we are able to communicate with one another.

1. A Brief Overview of 5G Networks and Cloud Computing
1. The Technology of 5G
   When compared to earlier generations of wireless technology, the fifth generation of wireless technology, often known as 5G, is intended to provide much higher data speeds, lower levels of network latency, and increased network stability. Because it runs on a higher frequency band, it is able to transmit vast volumes of data at a much faster rate than previous technologies.
2. Computing in the Cloud

The term "cloud computing" refers to the practice of providing computer services (including software, processing, and storage) through the use of the internet. Users are able to access resources whenever they need them from faraway data centers, which eliminates the requirement for any kind of local infrastructure.

II. Various Applications Within the Field of Telecommunications

1. Increased Capacity for Mobile Broadband (eMBB)
   The enhanced mobile broadband (eMBB) characteristic of 5G enables extremely swift mobile internet, which paves the way for uninterrupted video streaming, high-definition gaming, and speedy downloads. The cloud adds to this by providing the necessary infrastructure for hosting material and applications, which is something that was previously lacking.
2. Slicing of the Network
   Network slicing is a function that is made possible by 5G. This capability allows a single physical network to be partitioned into many virtual networks. The use of cloud computing enables more effective management of these slices by assigning resources according to demand.
3. The abbreviation for "virtualized network functions" is "VNFs."

The implementation of Virtualized Network Functions (VNFs), which include virtual routers and firewalls, is made possible by cloud computing. 5G networks may now take advantage of this technology. This not only cuts expenses but also makes it easier to rapidly deploy new services as well as boosts the network's agility.

III. Internet of Things and Smart Cities

1. Intelligent Systems in Place
   5G networks make it possible to connect a large number of Internet of Things devices in smart cities. These gadgets, which range from intelligent traffic lights to sensors for waste management, communicate with one another over 5G networks and make use of cloud computing to analyze and analyse the data they collect.
2. Monitoring from a Distance
   The high bandwidth of 5G networks and the data storage and processing capabilities of cloud computing make it possible to remotely monitor and manage multiple aspects of urban life, including energy use and public transit, amongst other things.
3. Healthcare and Remote Medical Consultations

3.1. Monitoring of Patients Via Remote Connection

5G makes it possible to remotely monitor patients' vital signs in real time from a distance, and the data may be transmitted safely to cloud-based platforms. This makes it easier to discover potential health problems at an earlier stage and enhances the quality of care provided to patients.

3.2. The field of telemedicine

Applications for telemedicine hosted on cloud computing platforms take advantage of high-quality video consultations made possible by 5G network speeds. Patients are able to establish connections with their healthcare providers from any location, and they can receive care and advice in real time.

3.3. The Analyses of Data

The processing power offered by the cloud facilitates advancements in both the field of medical research and data analysis. Cloud computing enables researchers to process massive datasets more quickly, which can speed up the discovery of new medical treatments.

IV. The Entertainment Industry and the Media

1. Totally Submerging Adventures

   Immersive technologies like augmented reality (AR) and virtual reality (VR) require networks with the bandwidth and low latency that 5G networks provide. The content distribution, processing, and rendering for these experiences are all supported by the cloud's resources.

2. The Streaming of Content

   Cloud computing is necessary for the operation of multimedia streaming services such as Netflix and YouTube since it is used to host and distribute content to viewers. Streaming content on mobile devices will be of a smooth and high-quality with 5G networks.

3. Video gaming

The minimal latency that 5G provides will revolutionize how cloud games are played. Cloud gaming allows gamers to access and play graphically demanding games while experiencing minimal lag and outstanding graphic quality.

V. Manufacturing and the Fourth Industrial Revolution

1. Remote Controlled Activities and Observation

   Manufacturers now have the ability to remotely control and monitor industrial operations thanks to the combination of cloud resources and 5G connection. This improves efficiency, cuts down on downtime, and maximizes the exploitation of available resources.

2. The Practice of Predictive Maintenance
   Machines are monitored by Internet of Things sensors that are connected to 5G networks. The cloud is used to perform analysis on this data to determine when it is necessary to perform maintenance, hence reducing costly breakdowns and downtime.
3. Management of the Supply Chain

Cloud computing helps to streamline the operations of supply chains. Data collected at a variety of places along the supply chain are compiled and evaluated so that decisions may be made more effectively and operations can be improved.

VI. Agriculture as well as Agricultural Precision

1. Remote Observation of the Crops
   IoT sensors deployed in the field send data to the cloud by communicating with one another across 5G networks. Farmers are able to remotely monitor the conditions of the soil, the weather, and the health of their crops, which enables precision farming.
2. Decision-Making That Is Informed By Data
   The data that is acquired from farms is processed by cloud-based analytics services. Farmers are better able to make informed decisions when they have more information regarding crop management, irrigation, and pest control.
3. Machinery that is Fully Automated

5G networks allow for the operation of autonomous machinery that can be operated from a distance. The use of resources provided by cloud computing facilitates the making of decisions and the coordination of autonomous farming equipment.

VII. Vehicles that Drive Themselves

1. Processing of Data in Real Time.
   A tremendous amount of data is produced by AVs, and this data is analyzed in real time by robust cloud servers. This guarantees that autonomous vehicles are able to make decisions quickly, which improves both their safety and their efficiency.
2. Mapping in High Definition and Localization
   The cloud is used to build and store high-definition maps for use with autonomous vehicles (AVs). These maps can be accessed by AVs, which enables accurate localization and navigation.
3. Support Provided Remotely

Autonomous vehicles are able to connect with distant operators using 5G networks in the event of hard scenarios or edge cases. Cloud computing resources enable remote control and provide assistance with decision-making.

VIII. Utility and Power Provision

1. Intelligent Electric Grids
   The monitoring and management of smart grids in real time is made possible by 5G networks. The cloud is used to perform analysis on the data collected from various sensors and devices, which ultimately results in more effective distribution of energy.
2. Management of Renewable Energy Sources
   In order to maximize the efficiency of the generation and storage of energy from renewable resources like solar and wind farms, 5G connectivity and cloud-based data analytics are required.
3. Administration of Water Resources

The management of water resources makes use of cloud computing resources, with data from Internet of Things sensors being transmitted through 5G networks. This guarantees that water is distributed effectively while also reducing waste.

IX. Retail as well as online shopping

1. Management of Stock and Supplies
   Retailers are able to check inventory levels with the help of IoT devices and 5G networks. Analytics performed in the cloud offer valuable insights into demand trends and inventory optimization.
2. Shopping with Augmented Reality (AR)
   Augmented reality retail experiences can now be supported by 5G networks. Before making a
   purchase, consumers can get a better idea of how a product will seem in their actual surroundings by using augmented reality (AR) apps on their smartphones.
3. Personalized Advertising and Marketing

Computing in the cloud makes it possible to analyze consumer data as well as customer behavior. Retailers can utilize this information to customise their marketing efforts, which allows them to give targeted deals, make product recommendations, and more.

X. Protection and Observational Capabilities

1. Upgraded Monitoring and Surveillance Cameras
   The video feeds from surveillance cameras can be streamed in high definition and in real time through 5G networks. These data are stored and processed by the resources provided by the cloud, which helps with video analysis, facial recognition, and object detection.
2. Analytics Predictive for Safety and Protection

Cloud-based analytics solutions analyse data from linked security systems and Internet of Things (IoT) devices. 5G networks are required for connectivity. The use of predictive analytics allows for the identification of prospective security threats and the alerting of workers in the security department in real time.

XI. Services Relating to Finance

1. Trading with a High Frequency
   5G is essential for the ultra-low latency connectivity required by high-frequency trading systems. Trading algorithms are processed using cloud computing resources, which also facilitates rapid trade execution.
2. The Management of Risk

Real-time risk management is made easier for financial institutions to handle with the use of cloud-based analytics and machine learning. The appraisal of credit risk, the detection of fraud, and the assessment of market risk all include the analysis of data derived from a variety of sources.

XII. Coordination of Labor by Distant Means

1. VDI stands for "virtual desktop infrastructure."
   Users can access their remote desktops using 5G networks with the help of cloud-based VDI solutions. Employees that work remotely can now access their work surroundings from any location thanks to this feature.
2. Conferencing with Videoconference

Video conferencing services that are hosted in the cloud are an absolute necessity for online teamwork. Communication over video and audio will have a higher quality and lower latency while using 5G networks.

XIII. Healthcare and Remote Medical Consultations

The combination of 5G technology and cloud computing has had a profound impact on the healthcare industry.

1. Monitoring of Patients Via Remote Connection
   The transmission of patient data to cloud platforms can now take place in real time thanks to 5G networks. The ability for medical professionals to remotely monitor patients enables them to deliver prompt treatment when necessary.
2. The field of telemedicine

Telemedicine solutions that are housed in the cloud are available through 5G networks. Patients now have the ability to consult with medical specialists from the convenience of their own homes by using high-quality video conversations.

XIV. Education as well as Online Learning

The fifth-generation wireless (5G) network and cloud computing both offer advantages to education and online learning.

1. Learning Environments Available Online
   5G networks make it possible to access learning management systems (LMS) that are hosted in the cloud. Students are able to have access to educational content and engage in online classes as a result of this.
2. Online Laboratories

Students are given opportunities for hands-on learning through the use of virtual laboratories that are housed on the cloud. Interactions and experiments in real time can be carried out with the help of 5G networks.

XV. Climate Science and Environmental Observation and Monitoring

1. Predictions of the Weather
   Cloud systems receive meteorological data transmitted from sensors connected to 5G networks. The accuracy of weather forecasts is improved by using sophisticated modeling and simulations run in the cloud.
2. Modeling of the Climate

Researchers who study climate use resources from the cloud to run complex climate models. In order to better understand and anticipate climate patterns, data gathered from a wide variety of sources is analyzed in the cloud.

XVI. Services provided by the government and intelligent cities

1. Governance of the Internet
   Cloud platforms are used to host a variety of governmental services, including the filing of tax
   returns, the application for permits, and the renewal of licenses. These services are accessible to the populace through 5G networks.
2. Administration of Traffic
   5G networks are essential to the connectivity of traffic sensors, cameras, and lights in smart cities. Data is processed via cloud-based technologies for real-time traffic control, which helps to reduce congestion as well as pollution.
3. The Management of Waste

Waste bins in smart cities are equipped with Internet of Things sensors that send data to the cloud using 5G networks. The collection schedules and paths are optimized thanks to waste management systems.

XVII. The Exploration of Space

1. Transmissions Received Via Satellite
   The fifth generation of wireless networking, or 5G, is utilized for telemetry and satellite communication to ensure that data from space missions is efficiently sent. Mission data is processed and stored using cloud resources.
2. Analyses of Data and Computer Simulations

Cloud computing is used to perform analysis and simulations on the data collected during space missions. This helps in the planning of missions, the analysis of data, and the conducting of scientific study.

XVIII. Concerns and Things to Take Into Account

1. Safety and Confidentiality
   The safety of data while it is being sent via 5G networks and while it is being kept in the cloud is of the utmost importance. Data encryption and other stringent security precautions are very necessary. In addition, concerns regarding one's privacy need to be carefully managed, especially when it comes to applications such as healthcare and surveillance.
2. Compliance with Regulations
   Applications that are used in industries such as finance, healthcare, and education are required to comply with certain regulatory criteria. It is critical to ensure compliance with all applicable data protection laws, as well as industry norms and standards.

3. Infrastructure of the Network
It is necessary to make significant investments in network infrastructure in order to fully exploit the potential of 5G and the cloud. These expenditures must include the deployment of 5G base stations and the development of data centers.
4. compatibility of functions
It is a challenge to make sure that products, software, and services that come from diverse manufacturers can all work together without any problems. In order to avoid compatibility concerns, standardization and open interfaces are absolutely necessary.
5. Competencies and the Workforce

The combination of 5G wireless networking and cloud computing calls for a workforce that is highly qualified and capable of managing these technologies. It is imperative that businesses make financial investments in the education and training of their workforce.

A disruptive force that will be felt across many different industries and use cases is the combination of 5G wireless technology and cloud computing. From telecommunications to healthcare, education to smart cities, these technologies are enabling advances that were formerly thought of as science fiction. They are also unleashing a new universe of possibilities, improving efficiency, and opening up new worlds of possibility.

It will be vital to address security, privacy, regulatory compliance, network infrastructure, interoperability, and workforce skills in order to unlock the full potential of these technologies as businesses and sectors continue to adapt to and harness the power of 5G and the cloud. The applications that are discussed in this extensive review shed light on the limitless prospects that 5G and cloud computing present, as well as the major role that these technologies play in transforming the way in which we work, live, and connect in the digital era.

5.1 Enhancing mobile experiences

The incorporation of 5G and cloud computing technology has resulted in a tremendous change in the experiences that may be had on mobile devices. Not only are these tremendous breakthroughs transforming the way we connect with one another, but they are also improving the ways in which we consume material, conduct business, and engage with the digital world. In this piece, we'll investigate the ways in which mobile experiences are being taken to new heights as a result of the convergence of 5G and cloud computing.

1. Enhanced Connectivity with the Use of 5G
   A new era of connectivity at lightning-fast speeds has begun with the advent of 5G, the fifth generation of wireless technology. 5G represents a significant advancement over its predecessors, such as 4G, thanks to its significantly faster data transfer speeds, which can reach multiple gigabits per second.
   Because of this lightning-fast connectivity, users of mobile devices will be able to enjoy interactions with programs and content that are both more seamless and more responsive. It is now possible to stream high-definition videos, participate in video conferences, and engage in online gaming on mobile devices without experiencing any noticeable lag or buffering. The reduced latency offered by 5G networks is especially important for real-time applications like augmented reality (AR) and virtual reality (VR), which require an instant reaction in order to provide users with an experience that is fully immersive.
2. Mobile applications and services that are powered by the cloud
1. Improvements Made to the Delivery of Content
   Cloud-based content delivery networks, often known as CDNs, make it possible for mobile users to access films, songs, and other forms of multimedia information in a timely and effective manner. Mobile users benefit from ongoing access to content of the highest quality from streaming services such as Netflix and YouTube, which make use of the storage and distribution capabilities offered by the cloud.
2. Availability That Is Constantly Available
   Cloud computing makes it possible for mobile applications and services to be accessible at any time of day. Users have access to all of their data, documents, and applications from any device with an internet connection, regardless of their location, which ensures increased productivity and convenience.
3. Individualization and the Incorporation of AI

The massive data processing capabilities offered by cloud computing enable the development of powerful AI systems. Because of this connectivity, mobile apps are able to provide personalized recommendations, which makes mobile experiences more tailored to the tastes of the individual user. The cloud and AI are making mobile interactions smarter and more intuitive, whether it's product recommendations for e-commerce websites, personalized content feeds, or voice assistants like Siri and Alexa.
3. The Revolution in Mobile Gaming

The convergence of 5G wireless technology and cloud computing has resulted in a dramatic shift in the mobile gaming industry.

1. Gaming in the Cloud
   Cloud gaming services such as Google Stadia, NVIDIA GeForce NOW, and Xbox Cloud Gaming (previously known as Project xCloud) would benefit greatly from the low latency and high bandwidth offered by 5G. The cloud now enables gamers to play high-quality games with intense graphics directly from the cloud, with very little lag and outstanding visual fidelity.
2. Playing on Multiple Platforms

Cross-platform gaming is made possible through the cloud, which enables players using multiple devices to compete against one another or work together in real time. The cloud makes it possible for players using different platforms to share the same gaming experience. This includes mobile devices, personal computers, and game consoles.

4. Mixed and Virtual Reality (Augmented and VR)

   1. Applications of Enhanced Augmented Reality
      AR apps like Pokémon GO have already showed the potential for merging digital and real-world experiences. These apps use augmented reality (AR). AR applications may now give real-time information and interactions thanks to the low latency provided by 5G, making these experiences even more immersive and responsive.
   2. High-Fidelity Virtual Reality

Experiences in virtual reality that are of a high quality require a large amount of computer power. The bandwidth provided by 5G and the cloud resources make it possible for mobile VR headsets to stream data-intensive material directly from the cloud, doing away with the need for extensive processing done on the device itself. The end result is virtual reality experiences that are easier to access and more economical for mobile users.

5. Working from a Distance and Working Together

   1. Virtual Desktop Infrastructure (often abbreviated as VDI)
      Virtual desktop infrastructure (VDI) solutions that are hosted in the cloud ensure that remote workers may access their work environments from any device that has access to the internet. This is now

absolutely necessary for companies to do in order to keep their productivity and operations running smoothly.

2. **Webinars and Video Conferences**

The use of video conferencing services that are hosted in the cloud has been an essential component in the growth of remote teamwork. Users of mobile devices with 5G connectivity can participate in real-time video meetings of a high quality and engage with one another regardless of where they are located.

6. **Always-On Connectivity for Internet of Things**

The Internet of Things (IoT) derives a significant deal of use from high-speed, low-latency 5G networks as well as the resources offered by cloud computing. Users of mobile devices can now take advantage of Internet of Things devices for applications such as smart homes, wearables, and health monitoring, all while enjoying uninterrupted connectivity and data analysis. As a consequence, life and health management become less labor intensive and more convenient.

7. **Wireless medical care and electronic medical consultations**

1. **Monitoring of Patients Via Remote Connection**
   5G makes it possible to remotely monitor patients' vital signs in real time from a distance, and the data may be transmitted safely to cloud-based platforms. The ability of healthcare personnel to remotely monitor patients allows for timely intervention while also lowering the frequency of in-person visits that are required.
2. **The Use of Telemedicine**

Telemedicine solutions that are housed in the cloud are available through 5G networks. It is now possible for patients to consult with medical specialists from the convenience of their own homes via high-quality video chats. This results in improved access to healthcare services.

The combination of fifth-generation wireless networks (5G) and cloud computing represents more than just an improvement in technology; it is also a transformational force that is transforming how we experience the mobile world. These technologies are improving every aspect of our mobile life, from ultra-fast internet and apps driven by the cloud to immersive gaming, augmented reality, remote work, and telemedicine.

Users of mobile devices can anticipate a future that will be even more integrated and interactive as a result of continued advances and growing usage. In this future, the possibilities for upgrading mobile experiences appear to be limitless. The synergy between fifth-generation wireless

(5G) networks and cloud computing is propelling innovation, connecting people with one another, and enhancing lives in ways that just ten years ago were unimaginable.

5.2 IoT and smart cities

The idea of smart cities, which are propelled by the Internet of Things (IoT), is radically altering the way people live in cities. Cities are becoming more effective, sustainable, and responsive to the requirements of their inhabitants by capitalizing on the connectivity and data-driven possibilities offered by the Internet of Things (IoT). In this essay, we will investigate how the Internet of Things (IoT) is influencing the development of smart cities in the future as well as the profound effects it is having on urban life.

1. **Internet of Things in Smart Cities**
   Definition of IoT: The Internet of Things (IoT) is a network of interconnected devices, sensors, and other things that gather and share data via the internet. In the context of smart cities, the Internet of Things refers to the process of integrating numerous devices and sensors into the urban infrastructure and systems in order to collect and evaluate data in real time for a variety of purposes.

2. **Improvements in the Management of the Infrastructure**
   Sensors connected to the internet of things are dispersed across cities for the purpose of monitoring and managing vital infrastructure. This includes keeping an eye on the state of structures including roads, bridges, and buildings to identify any necessary repairs. The city officials can more effectively prevent problems by using the data generated from these sensors, which in turn reduces the need for costly repairs and increases the level of safety.

3. **Making Efficient Use of Energy**
   The Internet of Things is utilized by smart cities to improve energy efficiency. Data is collected through sensors installed in streetlights, buildings, and transportation systems to ensure effective utilization of energy. For example, when there is no one around, the lamps can be set to dim, which saves energy and reduces costs. Thermostats in public buildings that are enabled with the internet of things modify the temperature settings based on occupancy, which further improves energy efficiency.

4. **Transportation that is Environmentally Friendly**
   Transportation networks that are supported by the Internet of Things are an essential component of smart cities. Traffic sensors and cameras offer information on the traffic situation in real time, which enables dynamic management of the traffic situation. The

Internet of Things is being used by public transportation networks to improve route optimization and passenger services, hence lowering congestion as well as air pollution. Charging facilities for electric vehicles are also connected, which encourages the use of environmentally friendly modes of transportation.

5. The Management of Waste

   IoT sensors are utilized in intelligent systems for waste management in order to improve garbage collection. Trash cans are equipped with sensors that detect when the containers have reached their maximum capacity. This allows waste collection services to take action only when the containers have reached their maximum capacity, hence limiting the number of unnecessary collections, as well as fuel consumption and emissions.

6. Safety and protection of the general public

   The Internet of Things improves community safety by making real-time monitoring and reaction possible. Central command centers are connected to video surveillance cameras for the purpose of providing real-time monitoring and a speedy response to incidents. Sensors that detect gunshots can send an immediate notification to law enforcement about any possible occurrences. In addition, the internet of things is utilized by fire and catastrophe monitoring systems in order to detect emergencies and quickly respond to them.

7. Keeping an Eye on the Environment

   IoT sensors measure the air quality, temperature, humidity, and noise levels in smart cities as part of the vital environmental monitoring that is required for smart cities. The data obtained enables towns to better pinpoint the origins of pollution, implement measures to reduce emissions, and improve the environment as a whole.

8. Participation of Citizens

   The Internet of Things (IoT) powers the platforms and mobile apps that smart cities use to encourage citizen engagement. Citizens have access to information in real time regarding a variety of topics, including public transit, the quality of the air, local events, and more. They are also able to provide feedback and report difficulties, thereby creating a communication channel in which citizens and local authorities can exchange information back and forth.

9. Healthcare and Electronic Medical Record Systems

   By providing remote patient monitoring and telemedicine services, the healthcare industry is able to benefit from the Internet of Things in smart cities. Wearable technology and sensors make it possible for medical professionals to remotely monitor patients' vital signs and deliver telehealth consultations using technology that patients

wear. This not only improves access to medical care but also lessens the necessity of going to appointments in person.
10. **Intelligent Power Grids and Utility Systems**

The Internet of Things is an essential component in the efficient management of smart grids and
utility systems. The use of smart meters and sensors enables real-time monitoring of energy, water, and gas consumption, which assists utilities in resource management and improves their ability to respond to power outages. This leads in reduced costs for both the providers of utility services and the customers of such services.

Concerns and Things to Take Into Account

The Internet of Things in smart cities offers a wide variety of advantages; nevertheless, there are also a number of obstacles and factors that must be taken into account.

1. Protecting Users' Privacy and the Data They Generate The huge amounts of data that are produced by Internet of Things devices need to be safeguarded to protect users' privacy and prevent illegal access. Strong precautions against cyberattacks are absolutely necessary.
2. **Management of Data:** Managing and analyzing massive amounts of data necessitates having superior data management and analytics capabilities. Cities require both the physical infrastructure and the specialized knowledge to efficiently manage these resources.
3. Investing in Infrastructure The incorporation of IoT into smart cities calls for a large financial investment in the form of technology, sensors, and network infrastructure.
4. Interoperability is a challenge since it requires making sure that different devices and systems from different manufacturers can function together without any problems. In order to avoid compatibility concerns, standardization and open interfaces are absolutely necessary.
5. Scalability Cities should prepare for scalability because the number of Internet of Things devices and the data that they generate will continue to expand in the future.

The Internet of Things has revolutionized city life by providing the power behind smart cities. Cities may become more efficient, sustainable, and responsive to the needs of their residents by implementing technologies that are interconnected with one another. The Internet of Things

(IoT) has the ability to continue expanding, which means that the future of smart cities will be one of continuous growth and progress. This will result in urban living that is smarter, safer, and friendlier to the environment. The Internet of Things (IoT) will reshape the urban landscape and help form a more connected and smarter future as urbanization continues to progress in cities around the world.

5.3 Industry 4.0 and manufacturing

The term "Industry 4.0," which is also commonly known as "the Fourth Industrial Revolution," refers to a significant change in the manner in which industrial activities are carried out. This game-changing trend makes use of cutting-edge technologies to build manufacturing systems that are intelligent, networked, and extraordinarily productive. In this essay, we will investigate how the fourth industrial revolution, also known as Industry 4.0, is radically altering the manufacturing industry and the tremendous effects it is having on productivity, quality, and creativity.

1. What exactly is meant by "Industry 4.0"?
    1. The Internet of Things (IoT), in which intelligent sensors and devices are implanted into machines and other types of equipment, enabling these items to collect and share data in real time.
    2. **Big Data and Analytics:** In order to provide insights and help with decision-making, advanced analytics tools process the massive volumes of data that are generated by devices connected to the internet of things.
    3. **Artificial Intelligence (AI) and Machine Learning:** The methods used in AI and machine learning enable machines to learn from data, improve processes, and make decisions on their own.
    4. **Cloud processing:** The cloud serves as a repository for data and applications related to manufacturing, and it also offers processing power and accessibility.
    5. **Additive Manufacturing:** Technologies like as 3D printing have changed the design and production of components, allowing for customisation and rapid prototyping. This has been made possible through additive manufacturing.
    6. **Augmented Reality (AR) and Virtual Reality (VR):** The technologies behind AR and VR make the processes of training, maintenance, and design more effective.

2. Important Changes in the Manufacturing Industry

1. **Smart Factories:** Industry 4.0 is paving the way for the creation of smart factories, which feature seamless communication between connected equipment, sensors, and other systems. These factories have the ability to respond quickly to shifting conditions and generate individualized goods while maintaining a high level of productivity.
2. IoT sensors monitor the state of machinery in real-time so that predictive maintenance can be performed. A reduction in the amount of time spent maintaining and repairing equipment, as well as associated costs, can be realized through the utilization of analytics technologies.
3. **Quality Control:** Internet of Things (IoT) devices and artificial intelligence (AI) driven image recognition systems analyze items at a degree of detail that is hard for humans to accomplish. This leads to an increase in product quality as well as a decrease in the number of defects.
4. **Management of the Supply Chain:** Supply chains that are supported by the Internet of Things provide real-time visibility into the movement of goods, which helps to eliminate bottlenecks, optimize inventory, and improve logistics.
5. **Energy Efficiency:** Data analytics are used by smart manufacturing systems to optimize energy usage, which in turn reduces costs and the negative impact on the environment.
6. **Customization and Personalization:** Industry 4.0 makes it possible to mass customize items by enabling on-the-fly alterations to manufacturing lines, which results in the creation of goods that are suited to the preferences of individual customers.
7. **Remote Monitoring and manage:** By combining IoT and AI, manufacturers now have the ability to remotely monitor and manage their machinery and processes. This capability is particularly important for companies who are involved in global supply chains.

3. **The Positive Effects of Industry 4.0 on the Manufacturing Sector**

1. **Increased Production Efficiency as a Result of Industry 4.0 Technologies:** These technologies streamline operations, which results in increased production efficiency. They also minimize waste and improve resource usage.
2. **Improved Quality:** The combination of automation and real-time quality control techniques ensures a consistent level of product quality while simultaneously reducing the number of defects.

3. **Cost Reduction:** Manufacturers can save money by using predictive maintenance, energy optimization, and effective resource utilization.
4. **Greater Flexibility:** Smart factories are able to quickly adjust to changing consumer demands, enabling a level of flexibility that was previously unattainable.
5. Product Development and Innovation Modern technologies, such as 3D printing and virtual prototyping, foster innovation and reduce the length of product development cycles.
6. **Empowerment of Workers:** Industry 4.0 does not replace human workers but rather enhances their capacities. Employees are given the ability to focus on more complicated tasks, while regular and repetitive work is handled by technology.

4. Obstacles and Things to Take Into Account

1. Data Security The increased connectivity as well as the increased generation of data both generate new threats. The protection of sensitive data and systems requires that manufacturers make significant investments in sophisticated cybersecurity solutions.
2. **Skills of the personnel:** In order to make the shift to Industry 4.0, your personnel needs to be highly skilled and capable of managing and maintaining cutting-edge technologies.
3. **Exorbitant Beginning Expenses:** The implementation of Industry 4.0 technologies frequently necessitates significant beginning investments in both infrastructure and instruction.
4. **Interoperability:** It is essential to make certain that various systems and devices are capable of interacting with one another in a seamless manner in order to avoid compatibility difficulties.
5. **Data Management:** Because of the enormous volume of data that is produced by Industry 4.0 systems, advanced data management and analytics capabilities are required.

The fourth industrial revolution, also known as Industry 4.0, is reshaping the manufacturing industry into one that is highly innovative, flexible, and efficient. The use of technologies such as the Internet of Things, artificial intelligence, cloud computing, and others gives manufacturers the ability to optimize operations, increase product quality, lower costs, and strengthen their competitive advantage in a global market that is continually expanding. Manufacturers who are willing to embrace the fourth industrial revolution and make the necessary adjustments are in a position to not only gain considerable benefits from this transformation but also define its destiny.

5.4 Healthcare, education, and more

Numerous industries, such as healthcare and education, and even more are being disrupted by technological advancements. As a result of this transition, novel solutions have been launched that significantly improve accessibility, quality, and efficiency in various areas. In this piece, we will investigate the ways in which technological advancement is transforming essential industries such as healthcare, education, and others.

1. Health care services
   1. **Telemedicine:** Telemedicine makes use of video conferencing and remote monitoring in order to deliver medical care to patients who are located in different locations. It broadens patients' access to medical treatment, particularly in outlying locations, and makes it possible for individuals to consult with healthcare professionals without having to leave the convenience of their own homes.
   2. **Electronic Health Records (EHRs):** EHRs digitize patient records and make them readily available to medical practitioners so that they can provide better treatment. This technology improves coordination between clinicians, lowers the risk of errors, and guarantees that patients receive the most up-to-date and accurate medical care possible.
   3. **Medical Imaging:** New imaging technologies, such as magnetic resonance imaging (MRI) and computed tomography (CT) scans, have brought about revolutionary changes in diagnosis and treatment. The technology of 3D printing enables the fabrication of patient-specific models and implants, which in turn helps to make surgical procedures more accurate and time-efficient.
   4. **Wearable Health Devices:** Wearables, such as smartwatches and fitness trackers, give users the ability to monitor their own health and share that data with medical specialists. The use of these devices encourages preventative care as well as early intervention.
   5. **AI-Assisted Diagnostics:** Artificial intelligence and machine learning algorithms have the ability to evaluate enormous databases of medical information. This can help in diagnostics, as well as in anticipating disease patterns and tailoring treatment strategies.
   6. **Drug development:** High-performance computers and data analytics help speed up the process of drug development by modeling the behavior of molecules and attempting to forecast the impact of these models' interactions. This results in a huge reduction in the amount of time and money required to develop new drugs.

2. Instructional

1. Education Made Available Worldwide Through Online Learning E-learning platforms, massive open online courses (MOOCs), and virtual classrooms have made education available to students all over the world. These platforms provide learners with flexibility and the ability to learn at their own speed, making education accessible to people from a wide range of backgrounds.
2. **Digital Textbooks:** The traditional textbooks are being phased out in favor of digital editions
that feature multimedia content, interaction, and information that has been brought up to date. Students are able to access their lessons on a variety of devices, and they can collaborate with their classmates and teachers without any difficulty.
3. **Gamification:** The use of educational games and simulations to increase both student engagement and the ability to remember new information. Students are encouraged to explore, experiment, and think critically when they are provided with an environment that is both fun and beneficial for learning.
4. **Virtual Reality (VR) and Augmented Reality (AR):** The technologies behind VR and AR provide learners an immersive educational experience. Students can virtually explore historical sites, dissect organisms, or undertake difficult scientific experiments, which improves both their grasp of the subject matter and their ability to remember it.
5. **Personalization Driven by AI:** AI algorithms assess student data and customize educational experiences to meet the unique requirements of each learner. This strategy makes it easier for educators to provide students with the specific support and resources they require, so guaranteeing that all students receive the assistance they require.

3. The environment and its sustainable development

The importance of technology in resolving environmental issues and achieving sustainability goals cannot be overstated.

1. Clean and Renewable Energy Sources Solar panels, wind turbines, and other energy storage technologies all contribute to the generation of clean and renewable energy. These technological advancements lessen our reliance on fossil fuels, help us fight the effects of climate change, and pave the way for a more sustainable future.

2. **Smart Grids:** Smart grids optimize energy distribution and consumption by making use of the internet of things (IoT) and data analytics. This technology helps to increase grid dependability while also reducing energy waste.
3. **Waste Management:** Internet of Things (IoT) sensors are used by smart waste management systems to monitor the amount of rubbish in bins. This allows for effective collection routes, which in turn reduces the amount of gasoline consumed and pollutants produced.

4. Means of conveyance

1. **Electric automobiles (EVs):** EVs are becoming more readily available and provide environmentally favorable alternatives to conventional gas-powered automobiles. Both the driving range and the ability to charge electric vehicles have increased as a result of technological advances in battery technology.
2. **Autonomous Vehicles:** The creation of self-driving automobiles and trucks is already underway, which promises to make transportation systems both safer and more efficient. These vehicles have the ability to ease congestion on the roads and increase the safety of driving on them.

5. Financial Institutions and Banking

1. **Mobile Banking:** Mobile banking apps provide users with convenient access to their accounts, allowing them to carry out transactions, pay bills, and manage investments directly from their cellphones.
2. **Cryptocurrency:** The rise of digital currencies such as Bitcoin and the technology known as blockchain is upsetting traditional financial systems. These cryptocurrencies offer a secure and decentralized means of transferring and storing value.

The use of technology has been a major contributor to progress made in a variety of fields, including medicine, education, and others. It gives people and organizations the ability to operate more efficiently, interact with people all over the world, and address critical concerns. The continued development of technology holds the possibility of bringing about a future in which the aforementioned fields will be more approachable, sustainable, and innovative than they have ever been.

Chapter 6

5G and Cloud in Business

The combination of fifth-generation wireless (5G) technology and cloud computing is a force that will revolutionize the commercial sector. When combined, these technologies, each of which is already rather advanced on its own, become much more formidable. In the course of this in-depth investigation, we will look into the ways in which the synergy between 5G and cloud computing is transforming the operations of businesses, making innovation possible, and driving the future of commerce. We will talk about the relevance of each of them individually, as well as their convergence and the impact they have on a variety of businesses.

1. The Importance of Fifth-Generation Networks for Businesses
1. Connectivity that is both Rapid and Dependablely
    The fifth generation of wireless technology, often known as 5G, offers speeds and reliability that have never been seen before. 5G represents a significant advancement over its predecessors, such as 4G, due to the fact that its data transfer rates are capable of reaching multiple gigabits per second. Because of this lightning-fast connectivity, organizations can have interactions with their data and apps that are both more seamless and more responsive.
2. Minimal lag between received and sent data
    The low latency offered by 5G is especially important for real-time apps, which demand an instant response from their users. This is helpful in fields where making decisions quickly is of the utmost importance, such as the financial trading industry and the autonomous vehicle industry. Because of the decreased latency, the capacity to process data in real time has been much improved, which has made it possible to make decisions more quickly.

3. Internet of Things and Communication Between Machines
   The Internet of Things (IoT) is a huge network of networked objects that can be supported by the increased capabilities of 5G. This is vital for a wide range of businesses, including manufacturing, agriculture, healthcare logistics, and agricultural production. The Internet of Things is capable of efficiently transmitting data through 5G networks, which leads to improvements in operational efficiency and decision-making.
4. Improvements to the Mobility of Workforces

5G makes it possible for remote workers to be more productive than they ever have been before. They are able to access their work environments, engage with coworkers, and operate apps that require a large amount of bandwidth without interruption from any location because they have access to high-speed, low-latency Internet. In a world where working from home is quickly becoming the norm, this is becoming an increasingly significant consideration.

II. The Importance of Computing in the Cloud to Businesses

1. Capacity for Growth and Versatility
   Cloud computing gives organizations the opportunity to adjust the amount of resources they use to match their current workload. The cloud offers the flexibility necessary to adapt to the ever-changing requirements of a business's software applications, as well as its storage capacity, computing power, and other requirements.
2. The ratio of profits to costs
   Cloud computing services use a mechanism known as pay-as-you-go, which removes the requirement for significant upfront investments in infrastructure. This cost-effectiveness is beneficial to firms of all sizes, but particularly young organizations and those classified as small to medium businesses (SMEs).
3. Availability of Access and Working Together
   The cloud makes it possible for members of a team to work together on a project in real time,
   regardless of where they are physically located. This accessibility is of incalculable value to companies that operate on a worldwide scale and to those who employ workers in faraway locations.
4. Continuity of Operations and Recovery from Natural Disasters

The data that is kept in the cloud is safe from the effects of natural disasters and may be backed up and recovered with relative ease. This ensures that there will be no disruptions to business operations and that any lost data can be recovered.

III. How 5G and the Cloud Will Converge in the Business World

1. Workforce that is more mobile and flexible
   As was said previously, 5G enables mobile workforces to be more productive by providing connectivity that is both high-speed and low-latency. When combined with the cloud, it enables workers who are not physically present to have seamless access to their work surroundings.
   No matter where a user is located, their virtual desktops and applications can benefit from increased responsiveness and accessibility when they are hosted in the cloud.
2. Data and Analytics Conducted in Real Time
   The reduced latency of 5G makes it an ideal candidate for real-time data analytics that are stored in the cloud. Real-time processing and analysis of data streams gives businesses the ability to obtain insights and make decisions based on that information on the fly. This is of the utmost importance in industries such as finance, where a difference of milliseconds can have a substantial impact on the results of trading.
3. Applications Utilizing the Internet of Things (IoT)
   IoT applications are given a significant boost by the confluence of 5G and the cloud. Data collection can take place on the device level, with transmission taking place across 5G networks to cloud platforms for further analysis. The real-time processing of data has numerous applications, including those in the fields of logistics, agriculture, and smart cities.
4. the optimization of the supply chain
   Supply chains can be improved with the help of 5G and cloud computing, which are both available to businesses. When paired with analytics performed in the cloud, real-time tracking of items through Internet of Things devices offers improved inventory management and optimizes delivery routes.
5. Customer Experiences That Are Completely Immersive
   When it comes to providing clients with immersive experiences, 5G's low latency and high bandwidth are absolutely necessary. Consumers are provided with a new level of connection and engagement through the use of augmented reality (AR) and virtual reality (VR) applications that are housed in the cloud. For example, retailers can provide augmented reality shopping experiences for customers,

allowing them to virtually try on things in their own homes before making a purchase.

6. Protection of Personal Information and Data

   Both 5G and the cloud provide increased security options, such as edge computing for detecting threats in real time. Together, they assist companies in safeguarding their data as well as the information of their customers. Nevertheless, it is necessary to continue to maintain effective security and privacy safeguards.

7. Creative Problem Solving and New Product Development

The confluence of fifth-generation mobile networks and cloud computing fosters creativity and quickens the development of new products. Cloud computing allows businesses to conduct simulations and models that require a significant amount of processing power, which cuts down on the amount of time and money spent on research and development.

IV. Repercussions for a Number of Different Industries

1. Wireless and wired communications

   5G and cloud computing will completely change how network infrastructure and service delivery are handled in the telecoms industry. Software-defined networking (SDN) and cloud-based network functions (NFV) make it possible to manage networks in a way that is more efficient, flexible, and cost-effective. Augmented reality (AR), virtual reality (VR), and driverless cars are just some of the new applications that can be supported by the faster and more reliable 5G networks.

2. Health care services

   Telemedicine, remote patient monitoring, and data analytics are all areas that will be revolutionized by 5G and the cloud in the healthcare industry. Transmission and processing of data in real time make it possible for medical professionals to remotely monitor patients and diagnose conditions in those patients. The ability to safely store and access patient records and medical pictures in the cloud further enhances the quality of treatment provided to patients.

3. Industrial Production

   Manufacturing is a sector that benefits greatly from the confluence of 5G and the cloud. In order to perform real-time data monitoring, predictive maintenance, and quality control, smart factories rely on Internet of Things devices that are connected to 5G networks and cloud-based platforms. This integration increases productivity, cuts down on unproductive time, and quickens the pace of product creation.

4. Storefront and Online Business

   Retailers may provide superior experiences for their customers by utilizing 5G technologies, such as augmented reality (AR) shopping and real-time inventory management. Personalized marketing, data analytics, and supply chain optimization are some of the functions that can be supported by the cloud. These technologies, when combined, generate both sales and satisfaction among customers.

5. The economy

   For high-frequency trading and real-time risk management to be possible in the financial industry, 5G and cloud computing are necessary. The combination enables data transfer and analytics to take place at lightening speeds, which ensures competitive advantages in the financial markets. In addition, solutions for mobile banking that are both accessible and secure can be found through cloud-based services.

6. Instructional

   The introduction of 5G networks and cloud computing is reshaping the landscape of the educational landscape of the future. The availability of high-speed internet and adaptable cloud resources are beneficial to online learning platforms, virtual labs, and individualized learning experiences. Even when they are in remote regions, students can easily access educational content and collaborate with one another.

7. Intelligent cities

   The management of traffic, the collection of waste, the monitoring of the environment, and other public services are all improved with the use of 5G and the cloud. IoT devices and sensors that are connected to 5G networks send data to cloud platforms so that the data can be analyzed and decisions can be made in real time. The implementation of these technologies results in improvements to the city's infrastructure and services.

8. The Exploration of Space

Even the exploration of space can benefit from the combination of 5G and cloud computing. Spacecraft equipped with 5G networks are able to transmit data to and from Earth at a much faster rate. Real-time data processing, simulations, and research are all made possible by using the cloud. This synergy is absolutely necessary for space missions, such as the exploration of Mars and the communication with satellites.

V. Obstacles and Things to Take Into Account

1. **Safety and Personal Confidentiality**
   The increased connectedness as well as the flow of data brings forth new worries regarding privacy and safety. To protect sensitive data and consumer information, businesses have a responsibility to make substantial investments in sophisticated cybersecurity solutions.
2. **The Infrastructure of the Network**
   The implementation of 5G networks as well as the scalability of cloud resources call for large investments in network infrastructure as well as data centers. These monetary commitments are something that companies need to be ready for.
3. **The capacity for cooperation**
   It is of the utmost importance to make certain that the products and systems sold by a variety of manufacturers can function in an integrated manner. In order to avoid compatibility concerns, standardization and open interfaces are absolutely necessary.
4. **Management of the Data**

Managing and analyzing the massive volumes of data that are produced as a result of the convergence of 5G and the cloud calls for capabilities that are advanced in the field of data management and analytics. In order to properly manage these resources, businesses require the infrastructure and the expertise to do so.

The convergence of fifth-generation wireless (5G) networks and cloud computing represents a technical synergy that will revolutionize the operations of businesses across a variety of industries and enable innovation. Because of this dynamic cooperation, mobile workforces are improved, real-time data analytics are supported, the acceleration of IoT application development is enabled, and immersive customer experiences are delivered. While technology may give a number of opportunities, it also brings with it a number of concerns around security and privacy that organizations will need to handle.

Businesses that see the benefits of this convergence and take steps to adapt to it will be in a better position to promote innovation, enhance operational efficiency, and maintain a competitive edge in a world that is becoming increasingly data-driven and networked. The results of this synergy are now plain to see, and it is expected that in the years to come, they will only become increasingly significant.

6.1 How telecom operators leverage 5G and cloud for competitive advantage

The infrastructure and services that connect the modern world are largely provided by telecommunications providers, who play an important part in this process. The arrival of 5G and cloud computing technologies presents telecom operators with a once-in-a-lifetime opportunity to innovate and secure a competitive advantage for their businesses. During this in-depth exploration, we will talk about how telecom operators may embrace 5G and the cloud to alter their businesses, improve their services, and keep a competitive edge in an industry that is rapidly expanding.

1. The Opening Statements
   Since the beginning, telecom operators have served as the central pillar of worldwide communication networks. They have made significant investments in the infrastructure in order to deliver voice and data services, which has driven connection all over the world. The landscape of telecommunications is, however, going through a significant shift as a result of the introduction of cloud computing and the coming of 5G.
2. The Impact of 5G on the Telecommunications Industry
1. Connectivity that is Extremely Rapid
   The next generation of wireless technology, often known as 5G, promises to deliver incredibly quick connectivity, with data transfer rates that can reach multiple gigabits per second. In the world of telecommunications, this is a game-changer since it enables service providers to provide customers and businesses with larger bandwidth and lower latency options.
2. Making the Internet of Things and smart devices possible
   The Internet of Things (IoT) absolutely need the increased capabilities that 5G can provide. It makes it possible to connect a wide network of Internet of Things devices, including smart homes, wearables, industrial sensors, and autonomous vehicles, amongst other possibilities. This presents an opportunity for telecom providers to build new revenue streams and business models by capitalizing on the trend.
3. Network Segmentation
   Network slicing is a new feature that 5G introduces. This feature enables network operators to
   divide their networks into numerous virtual networks, each of which is optimized for a different set of use cases. This flexibility is crucial for accommodating diverse services with varying requirements, such as huge IoT or ultra-reliable low-latency communication (URLLC), and it is important to note that these criteria can be met by URLLC.
4. Improved Capacity for Mobile Broadband

With 5G, telecommunications companies will be able to provide customers mobile broadband that is both streamlined and fast. This is essential for the provision of immersive experiences such as augmented reality (AR) and virtual reality (VR), as well as the support of apps that require a substantial amount of bandwidth such as online gaming and 4K video streaming.

III. The Importance of Cloud Computing in the Telecommunications Industry

1. Capacity for Growth and Productivity
   Cloud computing gives the telecommunications industry the ability to adjust the scale of their resources according to their needs, allowing for more effective management of both infrastructure and services. When it comes to meeting the ever-changing requirements of 5G networks and Internet of Things installations, this scalability comes in very handy.
2. Virtualization of Network Functions (also known as NFV)
   Based in the cloud Virtualizing network functions, which were previously only possible with hardware, is one of the capabilities offered by NFV to telecom operators. This move toward software-based solutions will speed up the deployment of new services while simultaneously lowering the cost of network maintenance and simplifying its process.
3. Software-Defined Networking (SDN), often known as "virtual"
   As a result of SDN's ability to separate network control and data forwarding, operators are provided with networks that are more programmable and agile. Dynamic network setup, traffic prioritization, and resource usage all become possible with SDN in the cloud.
4. Computing on the Edge

Through edge computing, cloud resources can be brought closer to end users, thereby lowering latency and enhancing the performance of applications that are sensitive to latency. Edge computing services can be provided by telecom carriers, providing real-time processing and data analysis for Internet of Things, augmented reality, virtual reality, and other applications.

IV. Gaining a Competitive Advantage Through the Use of 5G and the Cloud

1. Improvements Made to Applications and Services
   Innovative services and apps can be provided by telecom operators

by utilizing the high-speed and low-latency connectivity provided by 5G as well as the scalability provided by the cloud. Experiences that are immersive in AR and VR, communication amongst autonomous vehicles, and high-quality video conferencing are some examples of these technologies. Effective delivery of these services can be accomplished through collaboration between operators, content suppliers, and businesses.

2. Services at the Periphery

Enterprises can take use of low-latency edge services offered by operators if the operators first install edge computing capabilities at their base stations and points of presence. These services can support real-time analytics, decision-making that is powered by artificial intelligence (AI), and industrial IoT applications, and they can cater to a wide variety of industries ranging from manufacturing to healthcare.

3. Solutions for Internet of Things and Smart Cities

Cloud computing and 5G networks enable telecom carriers to provide complete Internet of Things (IoT) and smart city solutions. These systems have the ability to monitor environmental data, optimize traffic flow, manage public services, and increase energy efficiency; as a result, cities become more connected and sustainable.

4. "Network as a Service," also known as "NaaS"

Organizations can take use of NaaS, a cloud-based networking solution that offers organizations a network architecture that can be adapted to their specific needs and is available on demand. This gives companies the ability to more easily change their networks to meet their ever-changing requirements, thereby lowering their capital expenditures and improving their operational efficiencies.

5. Network Segmentation for the Purpose of Various Industries

The capacity to build bespoke network slices gives operators the opportunity to serve a wide range of industries, each of which has its own unique requirements. For instance, they are able to supply slices with low latency and great dependability for autonomous vehicles and robotics, while also giving slices with large bandwidth for augmented reality and virtual reality applications and gaming.

6. Data Centers at the Periphery

The construction of edge data centers at strategically located sites enables operators to efficiently process and store data in close proximity to end users. Online gaming, real-time financial trading, and video streaming are three examples of applications that absolutely require this feature.

V. Obstacles and Things to Take Into Account

1. Investments in Physical Infrastructure
   The deployment of 5G networks and the construction of cloud infrastructure both need for significant financial investments. The operators need to give careful consideration to the prospective return on investment when planning their capital expenditures.
2. Safety and Confidentiality
   The increased connectedness as well as the flow of data brings forth new worries regarding privacy and safety. The operators are responsible for the implementation of stringent cybersecurity measures in order to protect their networks and the data of their customers.
3. The capacity for cooperation
   It is necessary to ensure that devices and systems from different manufacturers can work together without any compatibility difficulties in order to give a unified user experience and prevent compatibility problems.
4. Observance of the Requirements

The regulatory contexts that operators must traverse can be quite complicated, notably the regulations governing data protection and privacy. Maintaining the confidence of one's customers and avoiding legal trouble both require strict adherence to these regulations.

The ability to use the confluence of 5G and cloud computing for a competitive advantage is uniquely positioned within the realm of telecom operators. Operators are able to bring value to both consumers and companies if they deliver innovative services, embrace edge computing, support IoT applications, and offer network as a service. However, they are also required to face difficulties relating to the investment of infrastructure, compliance with regulatory requirements, security, and interoperability.

Operators that are able to successfully integrate these technologies will be better positioned to transform their companies, improve the services they offer, and maintain a competitive edge in the fast expanding telecoms market. This is because the expansion of 5G networks and the development of cloud technologies are both expected to continue. A motivating force behind advancement and transformation is the ability of 5G and the cloud to innovate and challenge conventional approaches of conducting business in the telecom industry.

6.2 Startups and innovation in the telecom sector

The telecommunications industry, which is well-known for its incumbent companies that have been around for a long time and its complicated infrastructure, is undergoing a paradigm shift as a result of the rise of startups and novel technology. These disruptive technologies are transforming how individuals connect with one another, how organizations function, and how data is transmitted around the world. In this in-depth research, we will investigate the role that startups play in fostering innovation within the telecommunications industry, as well as the obstacles that they must overcome and the influence that their contributions have had on the sector as a whole.

1. The Opening Statements
   Because the telecom business has historically been dominated by huge corporations with considerable resources, it is difficult for new players to break into the market. On the other hand, the proliferation of startups has resulted in the introduction of novel ideas, adaptable approaches, and disruptive technologies that are transforming the industry. These new companies are at the forefront of innovation in a variety of fields, including the construction of new infrastructure, the provision of communication services, and the management of data.
2. The Function of New Businesses in the Field of Telecommunications Innovation
   1. Adaptable Strategies and Capability of Change
      The flexibility and responsiveness of startups in the telecommunications industry is well-known. They are able to quickly respond to the demands of the market and adopt creative ideas without being constrained by bureaucratic red tape, unlike larger enterprises. Because of this flexibility, they are able to experiment with new ideas and build technologies that are on the cutting edge.
   2. Technologies and Services That Cause Disruption
      Telecommunications startup companies are at the vanguard of the introduction of innovative technology and services that pose a threat to conventional forms of corporate organization. New technologies, such as Voice over Internet Protocol (VoIP) and cloud-based communication platforms, as well as novel solutions for the Internet of Things (IoT), are causing a revolution in the ways in which people connect with one another and share information.
   3. An Improved Experience for the Customer
      User-friendly interfaces, individualized services, and responsive support systems are some of the ways in which new businesses are working to improve the overall quality of their interactions with

customers. Their focus on ensuring that customers are happy and engaged creates a new benchmark within the telecommunications industry, which compels more established businesses to enhance the quality of the services they provide.

4. The Building of New Infrastructure

The adoption of 5G technology, the growth of fiber-optic networks, and the optimization of data transmission capabilities are all being driven by some startups that are at the forefront of innovation in the development of telecom infrastructure. Startups are increasing connection and improving network dependability by addressing infrastructure gaps and adopting emerging technology.

III. Principal Frontiers of Development for New Telecom Companies

1. Virtual Private Networks and Other Communication Services
   VoIP technology is being utilized by new companies in order to provide consumers and organizations with communication options that are more affordable. These services include voice and video calls of a high quality, as well as messaging and collaboration features, and they typically come at a lower cost than traditional providers of telecommunication services.
2. IoT Solution Providers
   IoT solutions are being developed by startups in the telecom industry for a variety of different industries. These solutions enable seamless interaction between devices, sensors, and networks. These solutions make it easier to collect data, conduct analyses, and automate processes, which gives organizations the ability to make more informed decisions and improve the efficiency of their operations.
3. Services Hosted in the Cloud
   A growing number of start-up companies are offering cloud-based services that make it possible for organizations to more effectively store, manage, and retrieve their data. Cloud platforms provide scalable solutions for the storage of data, the development of applications, and collaboration, which helps modern businesses meet the increasing digital expectations placed on them.
4. Protection of Computer Networks
   In light of the growing dangers to data security and privacy, companies in the telecommunications industry are working on building cutting-edge cybersecurity solutions to safeguard networks and sensitive information. These solutions, which include sophisticated protocols for encrypting data, algorithms for identifying potential

dangers, and protected communication routes, give companies and customers a sense of relief and peace of mind.
5. Optimization of the Network

Network optimization solutions that improve network speed, reduce latency, and boost overall connection are becoming increasingly important to the focus of new businesses. Startups may ensure a flawless and dependable user experience by deploying powerful network monitoring technologies, which allow them to identify and handle issues in real time, hence eliminating any potential disruptions to the user experience.

IV. Obstacles Facing Telecommunications Startups and Potential Opportunities

1. Sources of Financing and Investments
   Obtaining sufficient capital and investment is one of the key problems that new businesses in the telecommunications industry confront. The significant costs that are associated with developing infrastructure, conducting research & development, and expanding into new markets can be a hurdle for new businesses that are trying to establish themselves in an industry.
2. Observance of All Regulations
   Telecom businesses have a significant obstacle in the form of difficulty in navigating complicated regulatory frameworks and meeting compliance standards. A large investment of time, resources, and skill is required, in addition to compliance with industry-specific rules, licensing requirements, and laws governing data privacy.
3. The Rivalry in the Market
   The telecommunications industry is notoriously cut-throat, and well-established businesses hold the majority of market share. In order to achieve a competitive edge and attract a customer base that is committed to their brand, startups are required to differentiate themselves through the use of original value propositions, superior service offers, and innovative solutions.
4. Rapid Advancement in Technological Capabilities

Due to the rapid progression of technology, new businesses in the telecommunications industry face the task of constantly adapting to changing consumer demands, industry standards, and industry trends. It is absolutely necessary, in order to keep their relevance and competitiveness, to keep up with the latest technical breakthroughs and to incorporate those advancements into their solutions.

V. The Influence That New Telecom Companies Have on the Industry

1. An increase in both innovation and competition
   Established corporations in the telecom industry are being forced to boost their products, improve customer experiences, and invest in new technologies as a result of the increased competition and creativity that is being fostered by startups inside the industry. The expansion of the sector as a whole is being driven by this healthy competition, which is to the benefit of both customers and enterprises.
2. Increased Availability and Availability at an Affordable Price
   Telecom entrepreneurs are making communication services more accessible and more inexpensive for a wider audience by developing cost-effective solutions and using innovative technologies. This accessibility is particularly helpful for underserved populations and emerging economies, both of which typically have restricted access to traditional forms of telecommunications infrastructure.
3. Collaboration and Partnerships Within the Industry
   Some new entrants in the telecommunications business are teaming up with more seasoned companies in the field to forge strategic partnerships that capitalize on their combined areas of expertise, resources, and customer base. These relationships frequently result in the creation of novel solutions and the growth of service offerings, both of which are beneficial to both newly founded businesses and more established organizations.
4. The Formation of New Jobs and the Expansion of the Economy

The expansion of new businesses that provide telecommunications services generates new job possibilities across a variety of industries, including information technology, engineering, customer assistance, and business development, among others. The development of new jobs not only contributes to economic expansion but also to the stimulation of innovation in associated industries, which in turn helps to advance society as a whole.

VI. Prospects for the Long-Term Growth of Telecom Startups

1. 5G and Computing on the Edge
   Applications that make use of the capabilities offered by 5G and edge computing will continue to be investigated and developed by startups. Because of this, user experiences will be improved, data

will be processed in real time, and Internet of Things solutions will become more responsive and efficient.
2. **Internet of Things and Smart Cities**
The proliferation of Internet of Things and smart city efforts will provide chances for companies to build solutions that improve quality of life in urban areas, optimize infrastructure, and increase resource management.
3. **Maintaining Confidentiality and Safety**
Because of the growing concern for data security and privacy, new firms will continue to develop creative solutions to safeguard sensitive information and guarantee secure communication. These solutions will be designed to meet the needs of both enterprises and individual customers.
4. **Market Expansion and Reach Across the Globe**

When a startup has reached maturity and gained widespread reputation, it will look to broaden its presence in overseas markets. This expansion will spur worldwide competition as well as additional innovation within the telecommunications industry.

The introduction of new technologies, the promotion of healthy competition, and the broadening of access to various communication services are all positive effects that telecom start-ups are having on the industry as a whole. Even though they face obstacles such as funding, compliance with regulatory requirements, and competition in the market, startups are continually upsetting old business models and propelling the industry toward a future that is more interconnected, efficient, and user-centric.

It is abundantly clear that the telecommunications industry is dependent on startups for innovation and advancement, and the contributions that startups make have the potential to radically alter how people communicate and engage with technology in the years to come. We will continue to be witnesses to the evolution of this dynamic sector, and the role that startups play in determining the future of this sector will continue to be essential.

Chapter 7

Regulatory and Ethical Considerations

In a society that is becoming more digital and networked, regulatory and ethical considerations have taken on a far greater level of importance. The swift progression of technology, the ubiquitous use of data, and the worldwide reach of digital platforms have all brought up new difficulties and opportunities that need for a solid regulatory framework and high ethical standards. During this in-depth investigation, we are going to delve into the intricate details of the various ethical and regulatory considerations that pertain to the digital age. In this session, we will discuss the importance of having regulations that really work, investigate the ethical ramifications of new technology, and investigate the influence that these factors have on a variety of industries.

1. The Urgent Need for Legislation in the Age of Digital Technology
1. The Protection of Personal Information and Data
   The explosion of data in the digital arena, including information that is personally identifiable as well as financial and health-related, has given rise to concerns regarding the privacy and security of data. It is absolutely necessary to have regulations in place in order to protect individuals and companies from data breaches, unauthorized access, and privacy violations.
2. Antitrust Laws and Companies That Dominate Markets
   Concerns regarding anti-competitive behavior and monopolistic activities have been raised as a result of the enormous market domination acquired by digital platforms and tech giants. It is necessary to have regulations in order to guarantee fair competition and safeguard the interests of customers and companies with fewer resources.

3. The protection of one's own intellectual property and copyright
   The simplicity with which digital content can be copied and disseminated has given rise to a number of issues with intellectual property rights and violations of copyright. The rights of creators need to be protected, but innovation also needs to be encouraged, and regulations need to find that balance.
4. Dangers to Computer Security
   Hacking, ransomware attacks, and data breaches are just a few examples of the numerous cybersecurity concerns that exist in the digital world. It is vital to have regulations in order to define standards and requirements for the various cybersecurity measures that can be taken to protect critical infrastructure and sensitive information.
5. Harassment and hate speech in online forums

The proliferation of online platforms has also contributed to an increase in instances of cyberbullying, harassment, and hate speech online. Regulations are necessary to address these concerns and to foster an environment that is safe to use online.

II. The Importance of Ethical Conduct in the Age of Technology

1. Confidentiality and Informed Consent
   Fundamental ethical standards include protecting the privacy of individuals and seeking their agreement after providing them with appropriate information. Before organizations and individuals can collect and use individuals' personal data, they are required to first seek consent.
2. Openness and responsibility in all dealings
   Building trust requires complete openness regarding the data collection, processing, and dissemination processes. In the area of digital activity, organizations are required to be accountable for their actions as well as the decisions they make.
3. Fairness and equality in treatment
   Because of their potential to promote bias, discrimination, and inequality, it is imperative that digital technologies and platforms be free of these characteristics. It is imperative that efforts be taken to guarantee fairness and equal access for all parties involved.
4. The Influence on the Environment
   Because of increased energy consumption, increased technological waste, and increased carbon emissions, the digital era has a substantial influence on the environment. Ethical considerations highlight

the necessity of developing and implementing environmentally responsible technology and practices.
5. The Ethical Use of Artificial Intelligence and Automation

The responsible application of artificial intelligence (AI) and automation requires taking precautions to prevent the technologies from causing harm to individuals, displacing workers without offering suitable alternatives, or reinforcing existing prejudices.

III. Regulatory and Ethical Considerations in the Varying Sectors of the Industry

1. Health care services
   Regulations concerning patient confidentiality, such as the Health Insurance Portability and Accountability Act (HIPAA) in the United States, and the ethical concerns that surround them, are of the utmost importance in the field of healthcare. The advent of telemedicine, widespread use of electronic health data, and an increase in the number of mobile health applications have all created new ethical and regulatory hurdles.
2. The economy
   Regulations such as the Dodd-Frank Act and ethical considerations relating to responsible lending, consumer protection, and financial transparency are extremely important in the financial industry. The proliferation of fintech and virtual currencies has resulted in the emergence of new ethical challenges and regulatory complications.
3. Instruction
   Ethical considerations in the field of education include ensuring that all students have equal access to digital resources and maintaining the confidentiality of student information. Guidelines for the proper management of educational data are provided by regulations in the United States such as the Family Educational Rights and Privacy Act (FERPA).
4. Business in General and Online Shopping
   Both the retail and the e-commerce industries are facing regulatory problems relating to the protection of customers and the safety of their data. Fair pricing, open disclosure of product information, and responsible marketing are all aspects that should be taken into consideration while thinking ethically.
5. Content on the Internet and Social Media

Platforms for social media need to find solutions to problems relating to online harassment, the moderation of content, and users' privacy. The goal of regulations and ethical guidelines is to achieve a middle ground between unrestricted speech and the management of material with responsibility.

IV. New Technologies and Ethical Challenges to Consider

1. Artificial Intelligence, also abbreviated as AI
   Concerns about algorithmic bias, employment displacement, and autonomous decision-making are raised in relation to artificial intelligence (AI). In order to address these concerns, regulations and ethical frameworks are now being developed.
2. The use of biotechnology
   New developments in biotechnology, such as gene editing and cloning, raise ethical questions regarding the limits of scientific experimentation and the potential repercussions for humankind. These fields are regulated in an effort to ensure responsible governance.
3. Computing on the Quantum Level
   The possibility that quantum computing could be used to break encryption raises a number of moral questions that could have repercussions for people's right to privacy as well as their safety. To ensure the development and use of quantum technologies in a responsible manner, regulatory and ethical considerations are now taking place.
4. Augmented Reality (AR) and Virtual Reality (VR) both have their uses.

The virtual reality (VR) and augmented reality (AR) technologies have ethical implications involving issues of privacy, addiction, and the impact they have on interactions in the real world. The rights of users are the primary focus of regulatory efforts, along with encouraging responsible behavior.

V. Perspectives from Around the World on Matters of Regulatory and Ethical Concerns

The ethical and regulatory factors that are applicable in one jurisdiction may not be applicable in another. Even while there are certain principles that are understood by everyone, the interpretation and application of regulations might vary greatly. Even while there are international organizations and agreements with the goal of harmonizing some areas of law, such as the General Data Protection law (GDPR) in the European Union, there are still many obstacles to overcome in order to achieve worldwide consistency.

VI. The Function of Technology Corporations in the Existence of Various Regulatory and Ethical Frameworks

A significant number of enterprises in the technology sector, notably the most influential global tech giants, have a significant impact on the development of regulatory and ethical considerations. When it comes to establishing rules and norms, they frequently collaborate extensively with national governments, international organizations, and trade groups.

However, as a result of their power, concerns have been expressed over the possibility of conflicts of interest and the tendency for self-regulation to put the interests of corporations ahead of the public good.

VII. The Influence of the COVID-19 Pandemic on the Regulatory and Ethical Considerations

The COVID-19 epidemic has hastened the transition to digital platforms in a variety of industries, including healthcare and jobs performed remotely. This rapid transformation has resulted in major legislative and ethical issues, including concerns over data privacy, challenges with cybersecurity, and questions regarding the equal sharing of digital resources.

VIII. Finding a Middle Ground Between Creative Freedom and Moral Obligation

1. Flexibility in Regulatory Measures
   In order for regulatory frameworks to keep up with the latest technology developments, they need to be adaptable and flexible. Conversation and information sharing on a continuous basis are required for effectively addressing new difficulties.
2. Raising Awareness and Educating the Public
   It is imperative that the general public be made aware of the importance of data privacy, online safety, and digital rights. It is important that ethical considerations be incorporated into educational curriculum as well as public awareness efforts.
3. Collaboration Among Multiple Stakeholders
   Collaboration between governments, industrial players, civil society organizations, and academic institutions is required for effective regulation and ethical guidelines. This strategy, which involves multiple stakeholders, helps ensure that the interests of all parties are taken into consideration.
4. Unbiased Monitoring and Control

Regulations that are effective typically include independent oversight and enforcement systems, which are designed to hold companies and other groups accountable for the acts they take.

IX. Responsible Moral Leadership and the Obligations of Businesses

The importance of ethical leadership and being responsible for one's company cannot be overstated in the business world. Businesses that place a high priority on ethical conduct and social responsibility are in a stronger position to earn customers' trust and maintain their stellar reputations.

In this day and age, the responsible application of technology, as well as the defense of individual rights and the general public interest, are inextricably linked to the regulatory and ethical concerns that are taken into account. Ethical standards serve as a framework for guiding conduct and decision-making in the digital world, while effective regulation is vital to meet the complex difficulties that develop as a result of rapid technology advancements.

In order to strike a balance between supporting innovation and protecting ethical standards, it is essential for regulators, industry stakeholders, the general public, and members of civil society to have an ongoing communication with one another. The legal and ethical decisions that are made in the age of digital technology have a tremendous impact, which will shape the future of technology as well as society and the economy on a worldwide scale.

7.1 Government regulations and spectrum allocation for 5G

The rollout and implementation of 5G technology have been eagerly awaited due to the potential that it possesses to change not only internet connectivity and telecommunications but also a variety of different industries. Nevertheless, the role that government laws and spectrum allotment play in making this vision a reality is an extremely important one. In this in-depth examination, we will look into the significance of governmental laws and spectrum allocation for 5G, as well as the difficulties and factors to consider that are linked with them, as well as the influence on a variety of industries and on society as a whole.

1. The Opening Statements

    The fifth generation of wireless technology, often known as 5G, promises to deliver much higher data rates, lower latency, and a number of applications that will alter a variety of industries as well as everyday life. It is vital that governments all over the world establish thorough legislative frameworks and allot the appropriate radio frequencies, also known as spectrum, to fit the requirements of the

5G technology in order to fully tap into the promise of this new networking standard.
2. Regulations issued by the government and the significance they hold
 1. Management of the Spectrum
    The allotment of spectrum is regulated and managed by governments to guarantee that radio frequencies are used effectively and to prevent interference between various services and applications. This is absolutely necessary in order to achieve a stable and error-free 5G network.
 2. Protection and Assurance of Safety
    Consumers and organizations that use 5G technology will be protected by the safety and security requirements that are established by regulations. This includes criteria for equipment standards, restrictions regarding exposure to electromagnetic radiation, and regulations concerning cybersecurity.
 3. Installation of Necessary Facilities
    In order to facilitate the installation of 5G infrastructure, such as cell towers, base stations, and tiny cells, governments develop deployment standards. This includes things like zoning restrictions, the application process for permits, and environmental factors to consider.
 4. Protection of Personal Information and Privacy

In the 5G ecosystem, there are regulations that control the process of collecting, storing, and using individuals' personal data. Strong data protection laws are very necessary to ensure users' privacy in light of the massive amounts of data that will be generated by 5G.

III. The Assignment of Spectrum and the Significance of Doing So

The practice of allotting particular radio frequencies to a variety of services and consumers, such as 5G networks, is referred to as spectrum allocation. Because of a number of factors, effective spectrum allocation is absolutely necessary for the deployment and ongoing operation of 5G networks.

 1. Abilities and Performing Capacity
    Wireless communication relies heavily on spectrum as its primary resource. When adequate spectrum is allocated to 5G, this assures that it will be able to deliver high data speeds and low latency, which will allow it to satisfy the requirements of applications such

as augmented reality (AR), virtual reality (VR), and the internet of things (IoT).
2. Elimination or Reduction of Interference
Spectrum that has been effectively allotted reduces the amount of interference that occurs between the various 5G networks and other wireless services, so assuring a connection that is both stable and dependable. This is extremely important for industries such as healthcare and driverless vehicles, which rely heavily on having a constant internet connection.
3. Expansion of the Network
The efficient distribution of spectrum paves the way for the construction of 5G networks, which can now reach rural and underdeveloped areas as well. This helps ensure that everyone has fair access to the benefits offered by 5G technology.
4. Creativity and Rivalry in the Market

Because it makes it possible for new companies to gain access to the spectrum, a spectrum allocation procedure that is well-structured fosters innovation and competition. This results in a more extensive selection of 5G services as well as reduced prices for end users.

IV. Obstacles and Concerns Regarding Government Regulations and the Allotment of Spectrum for 5G

1. Coordination at the International Level
Spectrum is a limited resource, and the process of allocating it frequently requires international collaboration and cooperation. When it comes to ensuring global compatibility, which can be a difficult and time-consuming undertaking, governments have to collaborate with one another.
2. Striking a Balance Between Interests
Regulators have the responsibility of striking a balance between the competing interests of numerous stakeholders, including as consumers, industry, and telecom providers. It can be difficult to find a happy medium between fostering innovation and guarding the public interest in any given situation.
3. Addressing Concerns Regarding Safety
Concerns concerning security have been expressed in relation to the 5G technology as a result of the greater connectivity it provides and its dependency on vital infrastructure. In order to address these concerns, governments need to develop stringent legislation about cybersecurity.

4. Obstacles in the Installation of Infrastructure
There is a wide range of variety in the local legislation that govern the development of 5G infrastructure, such as small cells and base stations. It will be a huge task to streamline these standards in order to ensure that deployment will be efficient and cost-effective.
5. Protection of Personal Information and Privacy

Because 5G networks will generate an enormous quantity of data, governments will need to establish extensive data protection legislation in order to preserve the privacy of individuals. The goal of striking this balance is a difficult one.

V. Impact on a Number of Different Industries

1. Health care services
5G makes it possible to remotely monitor patients, provide telemedicine, and use Internet of Things devices in medical settings. In order to safeguard the health and personal information of patients, governmental rules need to establish the dependability and safety of these applications.
2. Driverless Cars and Trucks
For the development of connected and autonomous vehicles, the automobile industry is significantly dependent on 5G. In this quickly developing industry, regulations are absolutely necessary to guarantee people's safety and security.
3. Manufacturing and the Fourth Industrial Revolution
5G's low latency and high dependability are both beneficial to the manufacturing industry. It is imperative that regulations make it easier for 5G to be used in smart factories in order to improve production processes and automation.
4. The term "Smart Cities"
5G connectivity is essential for the operation of smart city applications including traffic control,
energy efficiency, and public safety systems. These smart city efforts would not be possible without the government's involvement in the form of legislation and spectrum allotment.
5. A formal education

The education industry leverages 5G for applications such as virtual classrooms and remote learning. Students and teachers need to have fair and equal access to high-speed internet, and regulations and spectrum distribution should promote this goal.

7.2 Data privacy and security concerns

Data privacy and security have become increasingly important concerns in the modern era of digital technology, affecting individuals, enterprises, and governments alike. It is now more important than ever to find effective solutions to these problems as a result of the rapid spread of technology, the exponential growth of data, and the constantly shifting nature of the threats that exist. In the following in-depth discussion, we will investigate the relevance of data privacy and security, the issues that they provide, and the techniques that are required to protect sensitive information in a world that is becoming increasingly linked.

1. **The Opening Statements**
   In the present day, where information is both a valuable asset and the cornerstone of modern technology, the protection of users' privacy and the security of their data are basic values. These principles include the security of personal and sensitive data, the prevention of unauthorized access, and the safeguarding of information against data breaches and cyberattacks. [C]onsideration should also be given to the prevention of illegal access. It is necessary for individuals, corporations, and governments to address issues regarding data privacy and security in order to preserve trust, protect secret information, and conform with the standards of regulatory agencies.
2. **The Importance of Keeping Personal Information Private and Safe**
   1. **Security of Individually Identifiable Information**
      People are willing to share their personal information with businesses and service providers, including their names, addresses, financial details, and medical history records, among other things. The implementation of data privacy controls guarantees that this information will be treated in a responsible and secure manner.
   2. **Dependability and a Good Reputation**
      It is essential for companies and organizations to uphold a good reputation for the security of their customers' and clients' personal information. The loss of confidence and reputation that might result from a data breach or violation of privacy can have serious ramifications, both financially and legally.
   3. **Observance of All Regulations**
      The General Data Protection Regulation (GDPR) in the European Union and the Health Insurance Portability and Accountability Act (HIPAA) in the United States are two examples of laws and regulations that have been enacted to protect individuals' personal information in a number of different countries. The failure to comply may result in financial fines and other punishments.

4. Protection of Protecting Intellectual Property
   The protection of intellectual property, trade secrets, and proprietary information is an extension of the precautions used to ensure the privacy and security of users' data. These measures are extremely important to companies because they allow them to keep their advantage over other businesses.
5. Protection of the Country

Privacy and security of data are absolutely necessary for ensuring the safety of sensitive government information as well as the nation as a whole. The effects of cyberattacks on vital infrastructure, military networks, and intelligence institutions can be devastating.

III. Obstacles and Causes for Concern

1. Violations of Privacy
   Data breaches are instances in which unauthorized parties get access to sensitive data. Cyberattacks, insider threats, and security flaws are all potential causes of these types of incidents. Breach of security can lead to the exposure of sensitive personal data, as well as financial loss and reputational harm.
2. Attacks made using digital means
   Cyberattacks cover a broad spectrum of potential dangers, from malware and phishing attacks
   to distributed denial-of-service attempts (DDoS). Data, networks, and systems are all fair game for these attacks, which typically have nefarious motives.
3. Dangers Coming From Within
   Threats originating within a company, such as those posed by workers, contractors, or business partners, are known as insider threats. These persons may purposefully inflict harm or exploit their access to data for improper purposes, such as financial gain.
4. The Changing Nature of the Threat Landscape
   The threat landscape is ever shifting, particularly as a result of the increasing sophistication of hackers. The introduction of new attack vectors, methodologies, and strategies poses a challenge to security solutions and necessitates ongoing adaptation.
5. The Encryption of Data
   Encryption is absolutely necessary for the protection of data at both rest and in transit. On the other hand, it can be difficult to manage the encryption keys, guarantee that encrypted data can be accessed when it is required, and stop unauthorized decryption.

6. Rules Regarding Personal Information

The existence of a wide variety of privacy rules all over the world, such as the General Data Protection Regulation (GDPR), the Health Insurance Portability and Accountability Act (HIPAA), and the California Consumer Privacy Act (CCPA), presents difficulties for businesses that operate in multiple countries. For compliance with these standards, a comprehensive knowledge of the laws protecting personal data is required.

IV. Methods for Maintaining the Confidentiality of and Protecting Data

1. An Evaluation of the Dangers
   It is important to conduct regular risk assessments in order to determine the value of data assets, as well as potential vulnerabilities and threats. A policy for the protection of personal data will be developed using this information as its foundation.
2. The Classification of Data
   Put data into categories according to how sensitive it is and how important it is. Because of this, businesses are able to distribute resources and put in place particular security measures in accordance with the value and risk associated with each type of data.
3. Restrictions on Access
   Put in place stringent access controls to make sure that only authorized people can access the data. This includes authenticating users, granting access depending on roles, and encrypting data.
4. Training in the Awareness of Security Risks
   Educate staff and users about the best practices for protecting data privacy and security. Phishing assaults and social engineering are two examples of the types of typical dangers that can be mitigated with the use of efficient security awareness initiatives.
5. The Encryption of Data
   Encrypt sensitive data both while it is being transmitted and while it is being stored. Data is protected from being accessed in an unauthorized manner using various encryption technologies, such as end-to-end encryption and data masking.
6. Software and Tools for Cybersecurity
   Use security software and tools to protect against cyberattacks and illegal access. Examples of such tools and software include firewalls, intrusion detection systems, and antivirus solutions.
7. A plan for dealing with incidents
   Create a thorough incident response plan that lays out the measures

that need to be taken in the event that there is a breach of data or a security issue. Having a clear plan can help limit the amount of harm that occurs and make it easier to respond quickly.

8. Adherence to All Regulations

Maintain awareness of applicable data protection regulations and ensure that you are in compliance with them. In order for businesses to demonstrate compliance with regulatory obligations, they could be required to hire a data protection officer (DPO) and conduct privacy impact assessments (PIAs).

V. The Importance of Technology with Regards to the Privacy and Safety of Data

The protection of users' privacy and the integrity of their data could be harmed as well as helped by recent advances in technology. On the one hand, technology advancements like artificial intelligence (AI) and machine learning make it possible for businesses to detect and respond to potential security threats in a more efficient manner. On the other side, technology also gives hackers access to new tools and strategies, which makes it increasingly difficult to keep one step ahead of the ever-evolving dangers.

VI. Evolving Technologies and the Effects They Have on the Privacy and Safety of Data

1. A distributed ledger system

   The use of blockchain technology allows for the safe storing of data as well as the conduct of transparent transactions. By creating ledgers that are decentralized and cannot be altered, it has the ability to completely transform the data security industry.

2. An Architecture Based On No Trust

   The guiding premise of Zero Trust Architecture is "never trust, always verify." This strategy needs continual verification of identity and devices and is based on the premise that an organization's network may be vulnerable to attack from both inside and outside the business.

3. Technologies that Enhance Privacy (also Known as PETs)

   The utilization of data for analysis is made possible by privacy enhancing techniques (PETs), such as differential privacy and homomorphic encryption, which do not reveal the raw data. While at the same time allowing for useful insights, these technologies assist protect the privacy of individuals.

4. Computing on the Quantum Level

Computing based on quantum mechanics may one day be able to crack currently used encryption protocols, which would be both a risk and an opportunity. Encryption strategies that are resistant to the effects of quantum computing are currently being developed by researchers.

VII. Predictions for the Data Industry Confidentiality and safety

1. Increased Strictness of Regulation
   It is anticipated that rules will become more rigorous as the topic of data breaches and privacy infractions continues to dominate the headlines. In order to remain compliant with the new regulations, organizations will need to make necessary adjustments.
2. "Privacy by Design" (in English)
   The implementation of privacy by design concepts, which integrate data protection into the production process of goods and services, is becoming increasingly common. The proactive incorporation of privacy protection measures into an organization's technologies and procedures.
3. A.I. and ML (Automated Learning and Machine Intelligence)
   When it comes to automating the process of threat identification and response, AI and machine learning will play a crucial role. These technologies will also be employed by cybercriminals, which means that defensive measures will need to be continually developed.
4. Identity That Is Not Centralized
   Individuals will have increased control over the information that pertains to them thanks to the use of decentralized identity solutions made possible by blockchain technology. This will result in less reliance on centralized databases.
5. Cooperation on a Global Scale

The protection of personal information and digital assets is a worldwide problem. In order to effectively manage global security threats and regulatory problems, it will be necessary for countries, corporations, and cybersecurity professionals to work together.

In this day and age, protecting one's privacy and maintaining data security are of the utmost importance, and their effects can be felt by individuals, organizations, and governments all over the world. A preventative and all-encompassing strategy is required for data protection in order to meet the challenges posed by constantly shifting dangers, a wide variety of rules, and the rapid advancement of technology. The proper protection of data will be important for sustaining trust, privacy, and the security of persons and key infrastructure in our increasingly interconnected world as technology continues to evolve at a rapid pace.

7.3 Environmental implications of 5G and cloud infrastructure

The introduction of 5G technology and the widespread use of cloud computing have fundamentally altered the ways in which we connect with one another, as well as the ways in which we work and live. These technologies bring about enormous benefits; nevertheless, there are also repercussions for the environment that need to be taken into consideration. The environmental impact of 5G and cloud infrastructure will be investigated in this in-depth study. Particular attention will be paid to energy consumption, electronic waste, and the possibility of achieving sustainability in this era of rapid technological advancement.

1. **The Opening Statements**
   A new age characterized by unparalleled levels of connectivity and computational capacity has been ushered in with the advent of 5G wireless technology and cloud computing. Real-time communication is made possible by this technology, which also lends its support to the Internet of Things (IoT) and improves the functionality of a wide range of applications, including telemedicine and driverless vehicles. Nevertheless, this transition to digital has important repercussions for the environment, which must be carefully considered.
2. **The amount of energy that is used**
1. **Computer Repository Facilities**
   Data centers, which are essential to cloud computing because they house the computers and other hardware needed to store and process data, are buildings that consume a significant amount of energy. Their business requires a substantial quantity of electricity for several functions, including lights, server upkeep, and cooling equipment.
2. **An increase in the volume of data traffic**
   More data-intensive applications and services are likely to become popular as a result of the advent of 5G technology, which guarantees extremely rapid connectivity and little lag time. This results in a bigger volume of data traffic, which places additional demands on data centers and the infrastructure of networks, which in turn leads to an increase in the amount of energy consumed.
3. **The Infrastructure of the Network**
   The introduction of 5G will necessitate the installation of a substantial amount of network infrastructure, which will include tiny cells, base stations, and towers. When it comes to data transmission and

reception, these components require a consistent source of power at all times.

4. Electric and Electronic Equipment

The use of 5G technology typically entails the utilization of power-hungry electronic devices that are also energy-efficient. Some examples of these devices include smartphones, laptops, and IoT sensors. The production of these devices, as well as their charging and use, all contribute to an increase in the amount of energy that is consumed.

III. Waste Electronic Equipment

Another environmental risk related to the rollout of 5G and cloud infrastructure is the accumulation of electronic garbage, sometimes known as "e-waste."

1. Decreases in the Average Lifespan of Devices

    A shorter device lifecycle is a result of the rapid progression of technology as well as the frequent updates that are made to devices that are compatible with 5G. This results in a greater amount of electronic trash because older devices are thrown away.

2. Becoming obsolete

    The introduction of newer, quicker gadgets that are compatible with 5G may cause older equipment to become obsolete. Even while there are initiatives to recycle electronic waste, a significant amount of it still winds up in landfills, where it contributes to the creation of hazardous waste for the environment.

3. Resources Made of Material

Extraction of raw materials and resources, such as rare earth elements, is necessary for the production of electronic device components including batteries, processors, and displays. The manufacturing of electronic devices is dependent on this process. The extraction process can have negative effects on the environment, including the destruction of habitat and the release of pollutants.

IV. Long-Term Viability in the Age of Technology

1. Efficient Use of Energy

    A number of initiatives are currently under way to enhance the energy efficiency of network infrastructure and data centers. This involves maximizing the effectiveness of cooling systems, making use of alternative forms of energy, and installing server hardware that is more energy-efficient.

2. Internet of Things and Smart Cities
   The Internet of Things, which will be made possible by 5G, has the potential to make cities both more intelligent and more efficient. Sensors that are connected to the internet can monitor and manage resources, cut down on wasted energy, and make urban planning more efficient.
3. Telecommuting and other forms of remote work
   The utilization of productivity tools that are hosted in the cloud and the ability to perform work from a remote location have the potential to cut down on the amount of energy that is used in offices. Working from home can be better for the environment if it results in less need for real office space and less traveling.
4. Cloud computing and virtualization of resources

Virtualization and cloud services make it possible to pool computing resources and dynamically allocate those resources, which significantly cuts down on the requirement for a vast physical infrastructure. Because of this, there is the potential for a more effective utilization of energy and resources.

V. Obstacles and Things to Take Into Account

It is necessary to take a comprehensive approach in order to address the environmental effects of 5G and cloud infrastructure.

1. Alternative Forms of Energy
   It is necessary to make the switch to renewable energy sources in order to cut down on the amount of carbon dioxide that is produced by data centers and network equipment. The environmental impact of energy consumption can be considerably reduced by the use of renewable sources such as solar, wind, and hydropower.
2. Efficient Use of Resources
   It is absolutely necessary to make efforts to increase the resource efficiency of electronic gadgets. In order for manufacturers to create products with longer lifecycles, they can design their products to be more durable, repairable, and recyclable.
3. Methods That Are Ecologically Sound
   It is important for the sector to have environmentally friendly policies and procedures, such as responsible recycling and disposal of electronic waste. Consumers should not be required to go through undue hassle or difficulty to participate in recycling programs for electronic garbage.
4. Energy-Efficient Appliances and Furniture

The production and widespread use of energy-efficient hardware, such as CPUs and components with lower power consumption, can help to reduce the amount of electricity that is needed by devices and data centers.

VI. Considerations for the Future

1. **Economy Based On Circulation**
   E-waste can be cut down significantly through the promotion of a circular economy, in which electronic products are created with the intention of being reused, repaired, and recycled.
2. **Regulations and Quality Assurance**
   The technological sector requires transparent norms and standards for energy consumption, the management of electronic waste, and long-term sustainability, and these should be established by governments and international organizations.
3. **Innovative Sustainability**
   It is essential for there to be ongoing research and innovation in order for the industry as a whole to be able to produce energy-efficient technologies and sustainable practices.
4. **Awareness of the Public**

It is vital to raise more awareness among the general population about the environmental effects of 5G and cloud infrastructure. Consumers have the ability to make more informed decisions regarding the products they purchase and to demand environmentally friendly practices from producers.

The infrastructure of 5G and the cloud have significant repercussions for the environment, the primary issues of which are the use of energy, the disposal of electronic waste, and the extraction of resources. It is possible, however, to lessen the impact of these issues and make the shift toward a digital future that is more sustainable if industry leaders, government officials, and individual consumers work together. The pursuit of sustainability in the information age is not only an ethical requirement from an ecological standpoint, but it also presents a chance to leverage technology for the betterment of the planet.

Chapter 8

Future Trends and Innovations

It is crucial for individuals, businesses, and societies in our constantly changing world to maintain a keen awareness of emerging fashions and technological advancements. If we are able to adapt, maintain our competitive edge, and seize new possibilities, it will be because we have a better understanding of the trajectory that technology, culture, and industry are following. This in-depth research delves into a number of the most consequential developments of the future as well as inventions that hold the potential to radically alter our world in the years to come.

1. The Opening Statements
   The rate of change in the world we live in today is unparalleled; it is being pushed by advances in technology, alterations in cultural norms, and problems on a global scale. Keeping abreast of emerging fashions and technological advances is more important than it has ever been. As we move forward into the future, there are a few important sectors that promise to promote both transformation and innovation:
2. Emerging Patterns in Technology
1. Machine Learning and Artificial Intelligence (also known as AI)
   In recent years, artificial intelligence (AI) and machine learning have made amazing advancements, and it is anticipated that this trend will continue. Numerous applications, such as predictive analytics and autonomous vehicles, as well as virtual assistants and recommendation systems, make use of the algorithms that are developed through machine learning. AI is also being utilized in the medical field to assist in the diagnosis of diseases and the formulation of treatment plans.

2. Computing on the Quantum Level
   The field of quantum computing is the next step forward in terms of processing capacity. It might be able to completely change the way cryptography is done, make supply chains more efficient, and answer difficult scientific issues that are beyond the capacity of traditional computers. Numerous corporations, including IBM, Google, and Rigetti, are now making large investments in quantum technologies.
3. Technology Based on 5G
   The deployment of 5G networks holds the potential to revolutionize internet connectivity and open the door to the Internet of Things (IoT). This will help applications such as smart cities, augmented reality, and driverless vehicles by bringing higher data rates, lower latency, and increased capacity.
4. Mixed reality experiences, such as augmented reality (AR) and virtual reality (VR)
   The technologies of augmented reality and virtual reality are causing a shift in the way we perceive the world around us. These technologies are finding applications in a variety of fields, ranging from immersive gaming and virtual tourism to professional training and remote cooperation.
5. IoT (Internet of Things)
   The Internet of Things (IoT) is rapidly growing, with billions of new gadgets and sensors being connected to it every year. The consequences of this network of networked devices extend to smart homes and smart cities, as well as to healthcare, agriculture, and the automation of industries.
6. The Technology Behind Blockchain
   The application of blockchain technology is not limited to cryptocurrencies like Bitcoin; rather, it has a wider range of potential uses. It provides a safe and transparent environment for storing data and conducting transactions, which makes it useful for applications such as management of supply chains, voting systems, and digital identities.
7. Computing at the Edge
   Computing at the edge puts data processing closer to the source of the data, hence lowering latency and enabling applications to run in real time. Applications such as driverless vehicles, remote monitoring, and the internet of things can benefit tremendously from its utilization.
8. Genetic engineering and other forms of biotechnology

It is anticipated that developments in biotechnology, such as methods for editing genes such as CRISPR, will soon bring about revolutionary changes in the fields of medicine, agriculture, and environmental protection. The ability to alter genetic material has significant ramifications for the prevention, diagnosis, and treatment of hereditary illnesses as well as for the enhancement of crop yields.

III. Developments in our Societies and Cultures

1. **Environmental Responsibility and Long-Term Sustainability**
   Sustainability of the environment and climate action are at the forefront of concerns for societies all over the world. The worldwide movement toward renewable sources of energy, electric vehicles, and the reduction of carbon emissions is pushing advances in environmentally friendly technologies.
2. **Telecommuting and the Lifestyle of a Digital Nomad**
   The COVID-19 epidemic was a driving force behind the increased use of remote work. It is anticipated that this trend will continue, with an increasing number of people taking up the lifestyle of a digital nomad and working from any location in the world.
3. **Increased Awareness of Mental Health**
   Awareness of mental health is on the rise, primarily as a result of the growing recognition of the significance of maintaining one's mental well-being. Telemedicine and smartphone apps designed specifically for mental health are helping to democratize access to mental healthcare.
4. **Acceptance of Differences and Participation**
   The demand for diversity and inclusion is transforming both the culture of industries and the cultures of individual companies. In an effort to develop an inclusive work environment and encourage diversity, organizations are putting into place new rules and practices.
5. **The Population's Increasing Age**

The average age of the world's population is increasing, which is driving innovation in fields such as healthcare, care for the elderly, and technology that promote healthy aging. These technologies include assistive devices and home automation systems.

IV. Trends That Are Particular to the Industry

1. **Healthcare and Online Medical Consultations**
   In order to expand access to treatment for patients and make it easier for medical professionals to provide care, the healthcare sector is

increasingly embracing telemedicine and other digital health technologies. The use of wearable medical technology, as well as remote monitoring and virtual consultations, is becoming increasingly common.

2. Electric vehicles (EVs) and environmentally friendly sources of energy

   The increasing popularity of electric vehicles is driving change in the automotive industry, which is currently facing disruption. Companies are investing in environmentally friendly transportation options, and governments are providing financial incentives to encourage the use of clean energy.

3. Electronic Commerce and Shopping Done Online

   The expansion of e-commerce is being fueled by improvements to online shopping experiences, the development of automated warehouses, and the introduction of expedited shipping options. The COVID-19 pandemic hastened the transition to shopping online for merchandise.

4. Financial Technology and Electronic Payments

   The banking and payments business is undergoing a transformation as a result of financial technology, sometimes known as FinTech. Convenient new financial services are being made available thanks to developments in areas such as digital payments, cryptocurrencies, and mobile banking apps.

5. Content for Streaming and Entertainment

   Streaming platforms and interactive content are becoming more prominent as part of the digital transformation that is now taking place in the entertainment sector. Augmented and virtual reality both present audiences with new opportunities to enjoy entertainment.

6. Educational Opportunities and Online Learning

Through the use of online courses, digital textbooks, and various educational technology platforms, e-learning is gaining popularity and penetration. These advancements are redefining the future of education and learning that continues throughout a person's life.

V. Obstacles and Things to Take Into Account

1. Morally Complicated Situations

   Artificial intelligence (AI), gene editing, and facial recognition technologies are all examples of innovations that present ethical problems regarding privacy, bias, and the responsible use of technology.

2. Safety and privacy online
   The dangers increase in tandem with the development of new technologies. Constant effort is required to thwart hackers' attempts to access sensitive data, computer networks, and physical infrastructure.
3. Being Fired From Your Job
   Automation and artificial intelligence have the potential to cause a ruckus in certain industries and eliminate some jobs. It is necessary to address the impact these changes will have on employment while also preparing the labor force for the upcoming shifts.
4. The Influence on the Environment
   Even while progress is being made in environmentally friendly technologies, the digital world still uses up enormous quantities of energy and resources. It is absolutely necessary to find a happy medium between the advancement of technology and the preservation of the environment.
5. Protection of Personal Information and Privacy

Concerns over the protection of personal information and the regulation of data usage are
developing as the prevalence of data in everyday life increases. The global community is moving toward the adoption of more stringent data protection legislation.

IV. The Path Ahead for Innovation in the World

1. Working with others
   It is absolutely necessary for individuals, businesses, and countries to work together in order to effectively handle global challenges and propel innovation. Projects that use open-source software, cooperation between the public and commercial sectors, and the exchange of information will continue to play critical roles.
2. Legal and Administrative Structures
   In order for governments to effectively manage developing technologies, protect people's privacy, and guarantee that ethical standards are followed, they will need to establish clear regulatory frameworks.
3. Acquiring the Necessary Abilities
   The workforce will need to adjust when new technologies become available. To maintain a competitive edge in the labor market, on going education and skill improvement are going to be absolutely necessary.
4. Long-term viability

The concepts of innovation and sustainability are intricately intertwined. In order to combat climate change and the decreasing availability of resources, one of the most important things that will need to be done is the development of environmentally friendly technology and practices.

This analysis just provides a glimpse into the future by discussing potential trends and developments that may emerge in the near future. In a world that is marked by rapid change and interconnection, the capability to adapt, to accept new technology, and to confront global concerns will be of the utmost importance. To ensure that the revolutionary power of technology is used for the benefit of individuals, organizations, and society as a whole, the pursuit of innovation should be driven by ethical considerations and a commitment to sustainability as we move forward.

8.1 What's next for 5G and cloud in telecom

A new age has begun in the field of telecommunications as a result of the confluence of 5G and cloud technologies, which has made it possible to achieve higher data rates, lower latency, and a variety of other cutting-edge services. When we look into the future, the future of 5G and the cloud in the telecommunications industry holds a great deal of promise and the opportunity for even more transformation. Within the scope of this in-depth study, we will investigate what the future holds for 5G and the cloud in the realm of the telecommunications industry, including forthcoming trends, technological breakthroughs, and the influence on a variety of other fields.

1. The Opening Statements

   The transformation of the telecommunications business is being driven in large part by the rise of 5G and cloud technologies. The fifth generation of wireless technology is called 5G networks, and it promises much better data rates and lower latency. Cloud computing, on the other hand, provides an architecture that is scalable and flexible for a variety of services. The convergence of these technologies is transforming the face of the telecommunications industry, with a particular emphasis on boosting connectivity, allowing new applications, and driving digital transformation.
2. New Developments in 5G and Cloud-Based Telecommunications
1. Integration of Edge Computing Technologies

   The convergence of edge computing, 5G networks, and cloud infrastructure is emerging as one of the most important developments in the telecommunications industry. Computing at the edge puts data processing closer to the source of the data, hence lowering latency and enabling applications to run in real time.

   This is especially helpful for use cases including Internet of Things networks, driverless vehicles, and smart cities. The establishment of edge computing facilities by telecom carriers is taking place in order to enable these applications.

2. Creating Slices of a Network

   The term "network slicing" refers to a notion that is important to 5G that enables a single physical network to be sliced up into several virtual networks, each of which can be customized to accommodate a different set of use cases. This technology enables telecom carriers to dynamically assign resources, which ensures that every service or application receives the required bandwidth, latency, and quality of service. It is anticipated that network slicing will be a game-changing technology for many different industries, including healthcare, manufacturing, and gaming.

3. Integration of Artificial Intelligence and Machine Learning

   The incorporation of artificial intelligence (AI) and machine learning (ML) into 5G and cloud

   networks is now underway with the goals of enhancing network management, optimizing resource allocation, and improving network security. While machine learning algorithms can automate operations such as network optimization and troubleshooting, AI-powered analytics can anticipate potential network problems and take preventative measures to address them.

4. Virtualization and Open RAN Networking

   Open Radio Access Network, or Open RAN, is a relatively new architecture that is being

   developed with the intention of decoupling the hardware and software of 5G networks. This strategy advocates for vendor-neutral solutions, which makes it simpler for telecommunications service providers to select components from a variety of suppliers in order to cut costs. Additionally gaining popularity is network virtualization, which encompasses software-defined networking (SDN) and network functions virtualization (NFV), and it enables better flexibility and scalability.

5. The Provision of a Variety of Services

5G and cloud technologies are making it possible for telecommunications companies to expand their service offerings beyond the conventional voice and data categories. This encompasses services like as connection for IoT devices, edge computing solutions, cloud-based security, and applications designed specifically for a given industry. The evolution of telecom businesses into digital service providers that offer a wide variety of solutions to a variety of industries is currently underway.

III. Developments in Different Types of Technology

1. The Evolution of 6G

   Research and development on 6G, often known as the sixth generation of wireless technology, have already begun even if the global rollout of 5G is still in its early stages. It is anticipated that 6G would enable data transfer rates that are even faster than 5G, support for applications driven by AI, and enhanced AR and VR experiences. There is a strong possibility that it will involve cutting-edge technology such as terahertz spectrum, quantum communication, and enhanced satellite networks.

2. Additional Safety and Protective Measures

   The protection of sensitive data is of the utmost importance, particularly as 5G and cloud
   infrastructure become an increasingly important component of essential services and industries. Future improvements in security measures will include the creation of secure 5G standards, as well as improved encryption algorithms and authentication procedures. It is of the utmost importance to safeguard vital data and infrastructure.

3. Methods That Are Ecologically Sound

   A source of worry is the high amount of energy consumption that is linked with data centers and network infrastructure. Future technological improvements will place an emphasis on environmentally responsible practices, such as the utilization of renewable energy sources to power data centers, the improvement of data center cooling systems, and the implementation of hardware that is more energy efficient. Many telecommunications companies have pledged their support for carbon-neutral and environmentally friendly energy programs.

4. Integration of Augmented Reality (AR) and Virtual Reality (VR) technologies

The virtual reality (VR) and augmented reality (AR) technologies will be increasingly closely integrated into the 5G and cloud telecom networks. Consumers will be able to have more immersive experiences, such as virtual travel and gaming, as a result of this integration. In addition, augmented reality and virtual reality will find uses in fields such as medical, remote collaboration, and professional education.

IV. Repercussions for a Number of Different Industries

1. Health care services
   Because of 5G's low latency and fast connection speed, telemedicine will experience tremendous expansion in the next years.
   The use of technologies such as virtual consultations, real-time data sharing, and remote monitoring of patients will improve healthcare delivery. Critical applications, such as robotic surgery, will receive support from the integration of edge computing.
2. Production (the Fourth Industrial Revolution)
   The implementation of Industry 4.0 best practices in manufacturing will be accelerated by the use of 5G and cloud technology. Connectivity with low latency and high dependability would be beneficial to the development of smart factories since it will enable automation, predictive maintenance, and real-time quality control.
3. Means of conveyance
   There will be breakthroughs made in areas such as driverless vehicles, networked infrastructure, and intelligent transportation systems in the transportation sector. 5G networks will make it possible for vehicles to connect with one another and with systems that regulate traffic in real time, which will improve both the safety of roads and the efficiency of traffic.
4. Referring to the Arts and the Media
   The entertainment and media business is going to undergo a sea change as a result of the high-speed data transfer offered by 5G. Streaming, gaming, and augmented reality/virtual reality experiences are going to grow more immersive while also becoming more accessible. The ways in which we engage with content and consume media will be altered as a result of augmented reality.
5. Agricultural Practices
   By using methods of precision agriculture, the agricultural sector will be able to take use of the benefits offered by 5G and cloud technology. Sensors connected to the internet of things, unmanned aerial vehicles (drones), and real-time data analytics will improve crop management, cut down on wasted resources, and raise agricultural output.
6. Instructional

E-learning and distance education will benefit from the increased bandwidth and computing power offered by 5G networks. An increase in connectivity will make it possible to hold classes online, create interactive content, and facilitate worldwide collaboration between students and teachers.

V. Obstacles and Things to Take Into Account

1. Installation of Necessary Facilities
   It is going to be a huge obstacle to overcome in order to bring 5G and cloud infrastructure to underserved and rural areas. It is vital, in order to bridge the digital gap, to ensure that everyone has equal access to sophisticated forms of communication services.
2. The Protection of Personal Information and Data
   Data privacy and security have emerged as two of the most pressing problems in recent years due to the growth of connected devices and the transport of sensitive information across 5G networks. It is absolutely necessary to ensure strong encryption, authentication, and compliance with all applicable data protection rules.
3. Standardization and interoperability
   When it comes to assuring compatibility across networks and devices, the establishment of global standards for 5G and cloud technologies is absolutely necessary. Interoperability enables frictionless communication as well as the effective utilization of available resources.
4. The Distribution of the Spectrum

Spectrum distribution is a complicated subject because there are many different parties competing for a restricted number of frequency bands. Spectrum must be allotted and managed in an effective manner in order to ensure that 5G networks will operate at their full potential.

VI. Potential Outcomes of the Future

1. Intelligent cities
   Cities will be transformed into intelligent and linked ecosystems by technology such as 5G and the cloud. The quality of urban life will improve with the implementation of smart infrastructure, lighting that is efficient with energy, traffic control, and real-time public services.
2. Major Steps Forward in Healthcare
   The field of telemedicine, as well as the practice of remote patient monitoring, will continue to advance. The delivery of medical treatment is set to be significantly altered by the proliferation of technologies such as surgical robots, wearable medical devices, and real-time data processing.
3. The Practical Applications of Augmented Reality
   The use of augmented reality will become widespread across a variety

of spheres, including but not limited to retail, transportation, the workplace, and the entertainment industry. AR glasses, for example, have the potential to provide users with real-time information as well as immersive experiences.

4. Cooperation on a Global Scale

Increased connection as well as improved tools for collaboration will make international collaboration in research, industry, and education much easier. The globe will be more interconnected than it has ever been before, surpassing the limitations of geographical locations.

There are many fascinating opportunities awaiting the 5G and cloud computing industries in the not-too-distant future. Not only are these technologies altering the way in which we connect with one another, but they are also modernizing a variety of industries and increasing the quality of life for individuals all over the world. Collaboration, standardization, and a commitment to ensuring that the advantages of 5G and cloud technologies are available to all are essential to achieving success as we manage the obstacles and considerations connected with these advancements. The future seems promising, and the telecommunications industry will continue to be a major influence in the world that will be created in the future.

8.2 Predictions for the next decade

Our future is being shaped by factors such as global issues, social dynamics, and technological advancements, which are all in a state of perpetual flux. When we consider the next ten years, a number of significant patterns and forecasts begin to emerge, each of which provides a glimpse into the possible future of our world. In the course of this in-depth discussion, we will investigate forecasts for the coming decade, including topics such as developments in technology, society, the environment, and international politics.

1. The Opening Statements

    The subsequent ten years are going to be a time that will be marked by incredible change. Innovations in technology, alterations in cultural values, and urgent problems on a global scale are all factors that are likely to have an impact on our future. These forecasts provide a glimpse into the possible occurrences that may shape the course of events during the next ten years.

2. Forecasts Regarding Technology

1. Dominance of Artificial Intelligence (AI) in the World

    The field of artificial intelligence (AI) will continue to grow, eventually

being ingrained in many facets of our lives. Solutions that are powered by AI will become increasingly prevalent, and their applications will range from improved cybersecurity and advanced robotics to personalized healthcare and autonomous transportation.
2. The Revolution in Quantum Computing 2.
The once-niche technology of quantum computing will soon begin to have relevance in more practical settings. It will have a substantial impact on sectors such as encryption, the discovery of new drugs, and the modeling of climate change. There will be an increase in the number of early applications for quantum computing, and quantum communication may become more common and secure.
3. Hyperconnectivity and Sixth Generation Wireless Networks
The first step is already being taken by 5G. The following decade will see the beginning of the rollout of 6G networks, which will provide even greater data speeds and lower latency. Advanced Internet of Things applications, smart cities, and the beginning of a new era of augmented and virtual reality will all be made possible by hyperconnectivity.
4. Recent Developments in Biotechnology
Biotechnology will usher in a new era of revolutionary change in the fields of medicine, agriculture, and environmental protection. Techniques for editing genes such as CRISPR will continue to advance, paving the way for more targeted therapies for genetic illnesses and higher agricultural yields as a means of addressing concerns about global food security.
5. Self-Driving Cars and Trucks
Cars that drive themselves and other forms of autonomous mobility will gain greater widespread adoption. Urban regions will see a reduction in traffic congestion as a result of shared autonomous vehicles, which will also alter the way we think about individual automobile ownership.
6. The Internet of Things or Metaverse

The idea of the metaverse, which is essentially a communal and shared online place, is going to pick up steam. It will act as a central location for a wide variety of online activities, ranging from social networking and online gaming to the creation of virtual workspaces and educational opportunities.
III. Predictions Regarding Society

1. The Increasingly Old Population and Care for Seniors
   The increase in the average age of the world's population will spur innovation in fields such as healthcare, care for the elderly, and technology that promote healthy aging. For the purpose of making life easier for elderly people, "smart homes" and other forms of technological assistance will become increasingly widespread.
2. Increased Awareness of Mental Health
   The public's understanding of mental health issues will continue to expand, with the primary goals being the reduction of stigma and the expansion of access to mental healthcare. There will be a beneficial effect on mental well-being brought about by the introduction of telehealth services, mental health apps, and initiatives to reduce stigma.
3. Telecommuting and the Lifestyle of a Digital Nomad
   The COVID-19 epidemic was a driving force behind the increased use of remote work. A cultural movement toward digital nomadism, in which individuals can do their jobs remotely from any location in the world, is expected to take place in the workplace over the course of the next decade.
4. Awareness of One's Impact on the Environment
   The maintenance of environmental sustainability and the pursuit of climate action will continue to be primary objectives. The adoption of environmentally beneficial practices will be driven by innovations in clean energy, electric vehicles, and the decrease of carbon emissions.
5. The Reform of Educational Practices

There will be considerable changes made in the educational system. E-learning and online education will become increasingly prevalent, and digital textbooks, virtual classrooms, and educational technology platforms will rewrite the rules of how we acquire knowledge.

IV. Predictions Regarding the Environment

1. Dominance of Renewable Sources of Energy
   The use of renewable energy sources, such as solar and wind power, is expected to become the norm in the near future. The generation of electricity will become more sustainable in more countries, which will result in a reduction in emissions of greenhouse gases.
2. Carbon Dioxide Sequestration and Utilization
   The development of technologies that can capture and use carbon will play an increasingly important role in the fight against climate

change. The amounts of carbon dioxide in the atmosphere can be lowered with the help of developments in carbon sequestration and conversion technologies.
3. Agriculture that is Sustainable
Sustainable agricultural practices will gain traction as a means of addressing issues relating to food security. Agricultural practices such as precision farming, vertical farming, and organic farming will gain increasing popularity.
4. The protection of biological variety

The work that is being done to preserve and restore biodiversity will pick up its pace. The protection of ecosystems, habitats for species, and key areas with a high concentration of biodiversity will be the primary focus of conservation efforts.
V. Predictions for the Entire World

1. Preparation for Epidemics of Disease
As a result of the COVID-19 pandemic, ensuring that the world is ready for any subsequent pandemics will become a top priority. An increase will be made in investments made in healthcare infrastructure, the development of vaccines, and international cooperation.
2. Shifts in the Geopolitical Landscape
The dynamics of geopolitics will continue to develop in the future. It is possible that the current balance of power in the world will shift, with rising economies gaining importance. In order to effectively solve global concerns, multilateral diplomacy and international cooperation will be essential.
3. The Use of Artificial Intelligence in Armed Conflict
Concerns over ethics and safety will arise as a result of the employment of AI and autonomous weaponry in combat. Intensification of international legislation and discussions surrounding the use of AI in armed combat.
4. The Exploration of Space

A brand new age will begin for the exploration of space. Our comprehension of the cosmos will be fundamentally altered as a result of human exploration of Mars, the construction of permanent human settlements on the moon, and the growth of space tourism.
VI. Obstacles and Things to Take Into Account

1. Morally Complicated Situations
   The increasing prevalence of artificial intelligence (AI), biotechnology, and AI-driven warfare poses ethical problems around privacy, fairness, and the appropriate application of technology.
2. Safety and privacy online
   The likelihood of cyberattacks and data breaches increases along with the progression of technology. The constant challenge that is protecting key infrastructure and data from being compromised by cyberattacks.
3. Being Fired From Your Job
   Automation and artificial intelligence have the potential to cause a ruckus in certain industries and eliminate some jobs. It is necessary to address the impact these changes will have on employment while also preparing the labor force for the upcoming shifts.
4. Protecting the Privacy of Personal Information

Concerns over the protection of personal information and the regulation of data usage are
developing as the prevalence of data in everyday life increases. The global community is moving toward the adoption of more stringent data protection legislation.

As a result of developments in technology, society, and the environment, the next ten years provide a wealth of opportunities and prospects for our collective future. As we negotiate the challenges and opportunities that lie ahead of us, the key to success will be a strategy that is proactive and thorough, guided by ethical considerations and a dedication to sustainability. This will be the most important factor in determining our level of success. The world is on the verge of change, and the way in which these forecasts play out in our future will be determined by the efforts that we make together.

8.3 Emerging technologies like AI and blockchain in telecom

The merger of up-and-coming technologies like as artificial intelligence (AI) and blockchain is driving a deep shift in the telecommunications industry, which is currently in the midst of this change. These breakthroughs are redefining the management of telecommunications networks, the delivery of services, and the enhancement of client experiences.

In this in-depth examination, we will investigate the impact that AI and Blockchain will have on the telecommunications business, as well as the applications of these technologies and the likelihood of additional shake-ups in the field.

1. The Opening Statements
   The telecommunications business is no stranger to technological advancement, having gone through the process of transitioning from traditional landline systems to contemporary mobile networks. The implementation of cutting-edge technology like artificial intelligence and blockchain will bring about the subsequent wave of transformation. These developments hold the potential to make telecommunications services more user-friendly, safe, and focused on the client.
2. The Importance of Synthetic Intelligence to the Telecommunications Industry

The discipline of computer science known as artificial intelligence, which focuses on the development of intelligent machines that are capable of learning, thinking, and making decisions, is having a huge impact on the telecom business.

1. Methods for the Management and Optimization of Networks
   The use of AI is essential to maximizing the efficiency of network performance. Identifying network anomalies, predicting outages, and adapting network resources in real time are all tasks that may be accomplished with the help of machine learning algorithms, which evaluate large volumes of data. Because of this, the reliability of the services and the effectiveness of the network have both increased.
2. Maintenance that is Predictive
   Predictive maintenance, which is powered by artificial intelligence, enables telecom operators to foresee breakdowns in network equipment before they occur. AI can find patterns in previous data that warn future hardware or software problems, hence decreasing downtime and maintenance costs. These patterns can be found by analyzing historical data.
3. Providing Service to Customers
   AI-powered chatbots and virtual assistants are quickly becoming standard components of customer care in the telecommunications industry. They offer immediate assistance, respond to questions, and can even fix basic technical problems. This not only makes customers happier but also decreases the amount of human assistance that is required for regular questions.
4. The Detection of Fraud
   Algorithms powered by AI are able to recognize irregular patterns of use and pinpoint instances of possible fraud or security breaches in

real time. This is absolutely necessary in order to protect customers as well as providers of telecom services from fraudulent actions.
5. Marketing Tailored to the Customer

Analytics powered by AI make it possible for telecom companies to analyze the behavior and preferences of their customers. Because of this information, businesses are able to provide individualized product suggestions and focused marketing campaigns, both of which will result in increased consumer engagement and income.

III. The Role of Blockchain in Telecommunications

The telecom business is facing a number of difficulties that can be addressed in a way that has not been done before thanks to blockchain, a decentralized and distributed ledger technology.

1. Protection and Verification of Identities
   The use of blockchain technology may make transactions and telecommunications networks more secure. It makes possible secure identity management and authentication, hence lowering the likelihood that unauthorized parties would gain access to critical information.
2. Protecting Personal Information
   The providers of telecommunications services manage massive amounts of sensitive client information. It is possible to utilize blockchain technology to provide immutable and transparent records of data exchanges. This can ensure data privacy and compliance with legislation such as the General Data Protection Regulation (GDPR).
3. International Calls and Billing
   By generating an immutable ledger of call and data consumption, blockchain technology has the potential to make the complicated process of international roaming significantly simpler. This results in fewer client disputes and increases the transparency of their billing.
4. Electronically Signed Binding Contracts

The use of "smart contracts," which are agreements that can carry out their own terms and have those terms directly encoded into code, can automate a variety of telecom procedures. For instance, they are able to automatically manage pricing and bandwidth allocation, hence removing the need for any kind of manual intervention.

IV. The Interaction of AI and Blockchain in the Telecommunications Industry

1. Improvements to Safety Measures
   The combination of artificial intelligence and blockchain technology has the potential to deliver comprehensive security solutions. While AI can monitor network activities in real time and identify anomalies, Blockchain technology has the ability to safeguard data from illegal access and assure its integrity.
2. Methods for the Detection and Prevention of Fraud
   Telecom providers are able to develop reliable fraud detection and prevention systems by utilizing artificial intelligence (AI) for real-time monitoring of network traffic and blockchain technology for safe data processing. When suspicious behavior is detected, an automated response may be triggered, such as the freezing of accounts or the modification of security protocols.
3. Confirmation of One's Identity
   Identity verification solutions that are extremely safe can be provided by combining AI-based biometric authentication with the decentralized identity management offered by blockchain technology. To ensure that only authorized personnel have access to important telecom services, this is an absolutely necessary precaution to take.
4. Billing and Finalization of Transactions

Billing and settlement procedures can be automated using smart contracts driven by artificial intelligence. Blockchain offers openness and accuracy in invoicing, while artificial intelligence (AI) identifies disparities and resolves disputes, which together simplify complex telecom transactions.

V. Obstacles and Things to Take Into Account

1. Protection of Personal Information and Compliance
   The application of AI and blockchain technology in the telecom industry results in the production of massive amounts of data. It is crucial to ensure compliance with data privacy standards like GDPR in order to preserve the privacy of customers and avoid any potential legal concerns that may arise.
2. Capacity to Grow
   The scalability of artificial intelligence and blockchain solutions will need to be carefully maintained as telecom networks continue to grow and improve in order to accommodate increased data loads and more complicated transactions.
3. The capacity for cooperation
   It is of the utmost importance to ensure that the various AI and

blockchain systems can work together without a hitch. To stop the fragmentation of the sector, interoperability standards need to be developed and accepted by its participants.

4. A Lack of Competence

In order to successfully integrate technologies like AI and Blockchain, qualified individuals are required. In order to fully reap the benefits of these developments, providers of telecommunications services will need to make investments in personnel education and professional development.

VI. Prospective Applications and New Developments

1. Optimization of the 5G Network
   When it comes to optimizing the deployment and maintenance of 5G networks, artificial
   intelligence will play a vital role. It will guarantee an effective distribution of available resources as well as a high level of service.
2. Improved Online Safety and Security
   Artificial intelligence (AI) and blockchain technology will collaborate to produce highly secure telecommunications networks. Artificial intelligence will keep an eye out for potential dangers and flaws, while blockchain will guard sensitive data.
3. Simulated or Digital SIM Cards
   Users will be able to smoothly transfer between different telecom providers and networks with the use of virtual SIM cards based on blockchain technology, which will increase both flexibility and competition.
4. Integration of IoT Devices

AI and blockchain technology will make it possible to manage Internet of Things devices in a manner that is both more safe and more efficient, with features such as automated updates and secure data exchange.

Artificial intelligence (AI) and blockchain technology have ushered in a new era of innovation in the telecommunications sector. The combination of these technologies holds the potential to render telecommunications networks more customer-oriented, customer-safe, and energy-efficient.

It is essential to solve difficulties related to data protection, scalability, interoperability, and skill shortages as the industry continues to implement solutions based on artificial intelligence (AI) and blockchain technology. The combination of artificial intelligence and blockchain technology reveals a potential future for the telecommunications industry in which networks are more intelligent, services are more reliable, and customers are better protected.

Chapter 9

Conclusion

A tectonic change has been set in motion within the telecoms sector as a direct result of the convergence of 5G and cloud technologies. This change is redefining the manner in which we interact with one another, communicate with one another, and work together in ways that were formerly the domain of science fiction. This dynamic duo's influence is felt far beyond the realm of the telecommunications industry, permeating practically every aspect of modern business and everyday life.

In this all-encompassing conclusion, we will examine the tremendous changes that 5G and the cloud have brought, the potential that they have unlocked, the problems that they have provided, and the roadmap for the future. We will also reflect on the extraordinary voyage that we have taken through the world of 5G and the cloud. As we reflect on this revolutionary partnership, it is abundantly evident that the landscape of the telecommunications industry has been forever changed.

1. The Beginning of a Process of Change
1. The Revolution of Connectivity

    A sea change in connectivity has been ushered in with the advent of 5G technology. The way we interact with the internet has been fundamentally transformed as a result of its lightning-fast speeds, low latency, and enormous gadget capacity. The ability to stream videos in 4K resolution, experience realistic augmented reality, or take part in virtual meetings with almost no lag time is quickly becoming the standard. Our personal lives have been impacted, and various businesses are entering uncharted terrain as a result of the recent increase in connection.

2. The Evolution of Edge Computing
   A new standard for data processing has emerged as a result of the combination of edge computing and 5G network technology. Edge computing guarantees that decisions and analyses are made in real time since it moves data closer to its original source. This has significant repercussions for applications of the internet of things, including smart cities and precision agriculture, as well as for autonomous vehicles and remote monitoring.
3. The Digitization of Everything
   The combination of 5G wireless technology and cloud computing has hastened the process of digital transformation in many different industries. The capabilities of this dynamic combination are being leveraged by a variety of industries, including healthcare, manufacturing, and logistics, in order to optimize their business processes, deliver new services, and enhance the consumer experience.
4. The Merging of Different Industries
   The convergence of businesses that had been operating independently has been made easier by the advent of 5G technology and cloud computing. For instance, the automobile sector and the telecommunications industry have collaborated to pioneer the development of driverless vehicles. The capabilities of this alliance are driving collaboration between the healthcare and information technology sectors on remote surgery and telemedicine.
5. Connectivity on a Global Scale

The combination of 5G and cloud computing is bringing a level of global connectivity not seen before. It is eliminating geographical barriers, making it possible for people all over the world to work together, and increasing the number of opportunities in education, healthcare, and business. The dream of a world that is interconnected on a global scale is quickly becoming a reality.

II. The Unleashing of Opportunities

1. Improvements to the Experience of the User
   The digital experiences of consumers are being improved, and now include everything from interactive instructional platforms to immersive forms of entertainment. These experiences have become more accessible and engaging as a result of the fast data rates provided by 5G and the processing power provided by the cloud.
2. Internet of Things and Smart Cities
   The rapid spread of the Internet of Things is being driven in large

part by the combination of 5G and cloud computing. The Internet of Things (IoT) has immense potential, delivering better resource management, higher quality of life, and more sustainable practices. This promise can be seen everywhere, from smart cities to connected equipment in agriculture, logistics, and healthcare.

3. The Transformation of Health Care

   The use of telemedicine and remote patient monitoring is rapidly becoming more common, particularly in regions that have a shortage of medical professionals. As a result of the COVID-19 pandemic, the significance of this is amplified by the fact that cloud-based systems make it possible to conduct healthcare consultations virtually.

4. Smart manufacturing and the fourth industrial revolution

   Industry 4.0 is bringing about a renaissance in the industrial industry by combining technologies such as automation, artificial intelligence (AI), internet of things (IoT), 5G, and the cloud. The efficiency, adaptability, and environmental sustainability of smart manufacturing facilities are all improving.

5. Developments in Computing at the Edge

Computing at the network's edge is becoming an increasingly important component in 5G networks. Real-time data processing and analytics are being made possible as a result, which is beneficial for applications such as autonomous vehicles, the internet of things, and augmented reality. A brand new era of innovation is about to begin as a direct result of this tendency.

III. Difficulties and Complicated Situations

1. Installation of Necessary Facilities

   There is still a great amount of difficulty involved in bringing 5G and cloud infrastructure to underserved and remote places. It is essential to bridge the digital divide in order to guarantee that everyone has equal access to these game-changing technologies.

2. The Protection of Personal Information and Data

   The ever-increasing amount of data that travels over these networks necessitates the implementation of stringent data privacy and security protocols. It is absolutely necessary to have more stringent rules and compliance frameworks in order to protect sensitive information.

3. The Distribution of Frequencies

   Spectrum must be effectively allotted and managed in order for 5G networks to be successful. In order to avoid interference and

spectrum depletion, this work, which is somewhat complicated, needs to be coordinated on a worldwide level.
4. Standardization and interoperability are both important
The establishment of worldwide standards for fifth-generation (5G) and cloud technologies is absolutely necessary in order to guarantee the interoperability of networks and devices. Because of this, communication is streamlined, and resources may be utilized effectively.
5. Deficiencies in Skill and Talent

A staff with the necessary skills is required in order to successfully implement and manage cloud and 5G technologies. The need for specialists who are able to develop, execute, and maintain the safety of these complicated systems is expanding.

IV. A Blueprint for the Years to Come

1. The Continued Development of 5G
The rollout of 5G networks will continue around the world, and they will eventually reach many more locations, both urban and rural. The applicability of the technology will broaden, which will result in 5G being the new benchmark in the field of telecommunications.
2. A deeper integration of computing at the edge of the network
The integration of edge computing will become more robust, expanding its scope to include applications that rely on real-time data processing, such as industrial automation, remote surgery, and autonomous cars.
3. Improvements to the Safety Measures
Increasing safety precautions will be a primary emphasis of the telecommunications business. Protecting data and infrastructure will continue to be a primary issue, whether it's done through encrypted data transmission or security solutions based on blockchain technology.
4. Methods That Are Ecologically Sound
The concept of sustainability is gaining more and more significance. In order to lessen their impact on the environment, telecom companies are turning to renewable energy sources, improving the cooling systems in their data centers, and installing gear that uses less power.
5. Mixed & Mixed Reality (Augmented and Virtual)
The use of augmented and virtual reality experiences will become increasingly commonplace in the near future. These technologies will transform the ways in which we interact with the digital world

in a variety of contexts, ranging from education and virtual tourism to entertainment and gaming.

6. Cooperation on a Global Scale

Increased connection as well as improved tools for collaboration will make international collaboration in research, industry, and education much easier. The globe will be more interconnected than it has ever been before, surpassing the limitations of geographical locations.

The telecom business has seen a deep transition as a result of the confluence of 5G and cloud technologies, which has resulted in improved connectivity, industry convergence, and a wide variety of prospects. The road map for the future promises further expansion, increased security, and the integration of emerging technologies such as augmented reality and virtual reality. This is despite the fact that obstacles such as the deployment of infrastructure, the privacy of data, and the security of the system still exist.

It is abundantly evident, as we consider our trip through the realm of 5G and the cloud, that these technologies are more than just tools for communication; rather, they are generators of progress, creativity, and global connectivity. Not only has the advent of 5G and cloud computing revolutionized the telecom industry, but it has also altered the ways in which people work, live, and engage with the outside world. As we continue down this path of transformation, we must remember that teamwork, innovation, and a resolute dedication to a future that is better connected, more efficient, and more sustainable are essential to our success.

9.1 Recap of the synergistic relationship between 5G and cloud

The convergence of 5G and cloud computing will undoubtedly usher in a new era of technological innovation. It is a transformational alliance that has transformed the landscape of the telecoms industry, offering speeds, connections, and opportunities that have never been seen before. This article will review the extraordinary relationship between 5G and the cloud, focusing on how the two concepts may mutually benefit one another and propel innovation within the telecommunications industry.

1. 5G and the Cloud: A Powerful Partnership
1. Velocity and Internet Connections

    The speed and connectivity that are necessary for current applications may be provided by 5G networks because to their extremely rapid data transfer rates and low latency. 5G establishes a new benchmark for connectivity, whether it be through the transmission of high-definition video, the provision of power to Internet of

Things devices, or the facilitation of augmented and virtual reality experiences.
2. Capacity for Growth and Adaptability
On the other hand, the cloud enables both scalability and flexibility in terms of the management of data and services. It supplies the infrastructure that is required to store, process, and distribute the enormous amounts of data that 5G networks create.
3. Computing on the Edge

The combination of edge computing, 5G technology, and cloud computing makes it possible to perform data processing and analysis in real time. Edge computing helps assist applications such as autonomous vehicles and Internet of Things devices by bringing data closer to its point of origin. This in turn minimizes latency.

II. Synergy's Potential Uses and Applications

1. Improvements to the Experience of the User
User experiences have been revolutionized as a result of the combination of the speed of 5G networks and the power of the cloud. Users are experiencing interactions with digital content that are smooth and of a high quality, and these interactions can range from immersive entertainment to interactive instructional platforms.
2. Developments in Internet of Things (IoT) Technologies
The success of the IoT can be attributed to this synergy. Real-time data processing and connectivity are two benefits that come from using 5G and the cloud. These benefits may be seen in a variety of applications, including industrial IoT, connected agriculture, and smart cities.
3. The Transformation of Health Care
Because of the reduced latency offered by 5G and the storage and processing capabilities of the cloud, telemedicine and the monitoring of patients remotely are rapidly becoming the standard. Access to medical treatment is being made easier because to these advancements in technology, particularly in more rural locations.
4. Smart manufacturing and the fourth industrial revolution
The fourth industrial revolution, often known as Industry 4.0, is now taking place in the manufacturing industry. With the help of 5G and the cloud, automation, artificial intelligence, and the internet of things are making manufacturing processes more sustainable and efficient.
5. Developments in Computing at the Edge

Applications that rely on real-time data processing can now receive assistance from edge computing, which is quickly becoming a game-changer. Augmented reality, remote surgery, and autonomous vehicles are just some of the applications that could benefit from this.

III. Obstacles and Things to Take Into Account

1. Installation of Necessary Facilities
   It will be a huge obstacle to overcome in order to bring 5G and cloud infrastructure to underserved and remote places. It is essential to close the digital divide in order to guarantee that everyone has equal access to these game-changing technologies.
2. The Protection of Personal Information and Data
   The ever-increasing amount of data that travels over these networks necessitates the implementation of stringent data privacy and security protocols. It is absolutely necessary to have more stringent rules and compliance frameworks in order to protect sensitive information.
3. The Distribution of Frequencies

Spectrum must be effectively allotted and managed in order for 5G networks to be successful. In order to avoid interference and spectrum depletion, this work, which is somewhat complicated, needs to be coordinated on a worldwide level.

III. Standardization and interoperability are both important

The establishment of worldwide standards for fifth-generation (5G) and cloud technologies is absolutely necessary in order to guarantee the interoperability of networks and devices. Because of this, communication is streamlined, and resources may be utilized effectively.

IV. A Blueprint for the Years to Come

1. The Continued Development of 5G
   The rollout of 5G networks will continue around the world, and they will eventually reach many more locations, both urban and rural. The applicability of the technology will broaden, which will result in 5G being the new benchmark in the field of telecommunications.
2. A deeper integration of computing at the edge of the network
   The integration of edge computing will become more robust, expanding its scope to include applications that rely on real-time data processing, such as industrial automation, remote surgery, and autonomous cars.

3. Improvements to the Safety Measures
Increasing safety precautions will be a primary emphasis of the telecommunications business. Protecting data and infrastructure will continue to be a primary issue, whether it's done through encrypted data transmission or security solutions based on blockchain technology.
4. Methods That Are Ecologically Sound
The concept of sustainability is gaining more and more significance. In order to lessen their impact on the environment, telecom companies are turning to renewable energy sources, improving the cooling systems in their data centers, and installing gear that uses less power.
5. Mixed & Mixed Reality (Augmented and Virtual)

The use of augmented and virtual reality experiences will become increasingly commonplace in the near future. These technologies will transform the ways in which we interact with the digital world in a variety of contexts, ranging from education and virtual tourism to entertainment and gaming.

A game-changing collaboration in the telecommunications industry has been made possible by the complementary nature of 5G and cloud technologies. The combination of these two factors improves connectedness, opens up new prospects, and stimulates innovative thinking. Even while problems like the deployment of infrastructure, data privacy, and security still exist, the road map for the future promises to be a journey of expansion, advancements to security, and the incorporation of emerging technologies.

Not only has the advent of 5G and cloud computing revolutionized the telecom industry, but it has also altered the ways in which people work, live, and engage with the outside world. As we continue down this path of transformation, we must remember that teamwork, innovation, and a resolute dedication to a future that is better connected, more efficient, and more sustainable are essential to our success.

9.2 The transformative impact on the telecommunications industry

In recent years, the industry of telecommunications, which is frequently referred to as the backbone of the digital age, has undergone a paradigm shift that has caused significant change. The convergence of a number of different technologies and trends, such as 5G, the Internet of Things (IoT), artificial intelligence (AI), and the cloud, has been the driving force behind this transition.

These new advancements have not only remodeled the industry, but they have also had a significant influence on society, business, and the economy on a global scale. In this in-depth study, we will investigate the industry-altering impact that 5G will have, focusing on the most important drivers, problems, and opportunities for the future.

1. The Opening Statements
1. Technology Based on 5G
   The introduction of 5G network technology marks an important new phase in the evolution of the telecommunications sector. 5G has reimagined what is feasible in terms of network connectivity by providing data transfer rates that are comparable to those of light speed, low latency, and the capacity to link a massive number of devices all at once.
2. IoT stands for the Internet of Things.
   The Internet of Things has made possible the proliferation of a large number of networked devices and sensors that are able to produce and send data in real time. Because of this, telecommunications firms now have potential to provide connectivity and management services for Internet of Things devices used in a variety of industries, ranging from healthcare to transportation.
3. Artificial Intelligence, also referred to as AI
   As a result of their ability to improve network management, customer service, and data analysis, AI and machine learning have become indispensable components of the telecommunications industry. AI is being used to improve network speed, automate customer service, and anticipate potential problems with the network before they arise.
4. Computing in the Cloud

Cloud computing has completely altered the manner in which telecom providers manage data and deliver services. The infrastructure of the cloud makes it possible to implement solutions that are scalable and flexible, which in turn enables the quick deployment of new services and applications.

II. The Most Important Revolutionary Effects

1. Improved Overall Capacity of the Network
   A brand new era in terms of network performance has begun with the advent of 5G technology. Users will be able to enjoy smooth experiences thanks to data speeds approaching gigabit levels and

little latency. These improvements will allow users to enjoy high-definition video streaming, online gaming, and augmented reality applications, among other things.
2. Connectivity that is everywhere
5G networks are making it possible for a massive number of devices to maintain continuous communication. This is of utmost significance for the Internet of Things, as its sensors and gadgets necessitate connections that are both dependable and low-latency in order to communicate and share data.
3. Optimization of the Network
The performance of telecommunications networks is being improved with the assistance of AI
and machine learning. These technologies analyze enormous volumes of data in order to forecast and avoid any problems with the network, which ultimately results in networks that are more dependable and effective.
4. Changing Aspects of Business Models
Traditional phone and data services are being phased out as traditional telecom operators transition to new revenue models. As part of their strategy to diversify their sources of revenue, they are investigating potential opportunities in the areas of IoT connectivity, cloud services, and edge computing.
5. Computing on the Edge
The use of edge computing in conjunction with 5G networks makes it possible to perform data processing and analysis in real time at the network's periphery. Applications such as autonomous vehicles, augmented reality, and the industrial internet of things all require this information.
6. Increased Safety and Protection

The telecommunications industry is making significant investments in the improvement of security measures, particularly in light of the growing number of devices and data that are connected to their networks. This includes the implementation of sophisticated fraud detection systems, identity management platforms, and encryption protocols.
III. Difficulties and Complicated Situations

1. Installation of Necessary Facilities
There is still a great amount of difficulty involved in bringing 5G and cloud infrastructure to underserved and remote places. In order to

close the digital divide, it is essential to work toward ensuring equal access to these technologies.
2. The Protection of Personal Information and Data
The ever-increasing amount of data that travels over these networks necessitates the implementation of stringent data privacy and security protocols. It is absolutely necessary to have more stringent rules and compliance frameworks in order to protect sensitive information.
3. The Distribution of Frequencies
Spectrum must be effectively allotted and managed in order for 5G networks to be successful. Because of the complexity of this task, worldwide coordination is required in order to avoid interference and limited spectrum resources.
4. Standardization and interoperability are both important.
When it comes to assuring interoperability between networks and devices, having global standards for 5G and cloud technologies is absolutely necessary. Because of this, communication is streamlined, and resources may be utilized effectively.
5. Deficiencies in Skill and Talent

A staff with the necessary skills is required in order to successfully implement and manage cloud and 5G technologies. The need for specialists who are able to develop, execute, and maintain the safety of these complicated systems is expanding.

IV. Prospects for the Future

1. The Continuation of the 5G Expansion
The rollout of 5G networks will continue around the world, and they will eventually reach many more locations, both urban and rural. The applicability of the technology will broaden, which will result in 5G being the new benchmark in the field of telecommunications.
2. A deeper integration of computing at the edge of the network
The integration of edge computing will become more robust, expanding its scope to include applications that rely on real-time data processing, such as industrial automation, remote surgery, and autonomous cars.
3. Improvements to the Safety Measures
Increasing safety precautions will be a primary emphasis of the telecommunications business. Protecting data and infrastructure will continue to be a primary issue, whether it's done through encrypted

data transmission or security solutions based on blockchain technology.
4. Methods That Are Ecologically Sound
   The concept of sustainability is gaining more and more significance. In order to lessen their impact on the environment, telecom companies are turning to renewable energy sources, improving the cooling systems in their data centers, and installing gear that uses less power.
5. Mixed & Mixed Reality (Augmented and Virtual)

The use of augmented and virtual reality experiences will become increasingly commonplace in the near future. These technologies will transform the ways in which we interact with the digital world in a variety of contexts, ranging from education and virtual tourism to entertainment and gaming.

The strength of innovation and technology is demonstrated by the change of the telecommunications industry, which is being driven by 5G, the Internet of Things, artificial intelligence, and the cloud. It has ushered in a new era marked by increased connectedness, the diversification of business, and the possibility of having a good impact on a worldwide scale. Even while obstacles now exist, they are being tackled with the same innovative mindset that is driving the progress of the sector as a whole.

When we consider the revolutionary effect that these technologies have had on the telecommunications industry, it becomes abundantly evident that this sector is at the vanguard of the charge to mold the digital future. The possibilities are endless, and the path of innovation is still being paved, which holds out hope for a future that is better connected, more efficient, and more environmentally friendly.

9.3 The role of innovation and collaboration in shaping the future

The future of enterprises, society, and the world as a whole will be shaped in large part by two fundamental forces: innovation and collaborative effort. These two pillars of progress have moved humanity forward in many ways, from technological advancements to medical discoveries and transformational changes in business model paradigms. During this in-depth investigation, we will delve into the significant significance that innovation and collaboration have in molding the future, analyzing their impact on a variety of fields as well as the crucial interplay that exists between them.

1. The Influence of Inventiveness

1. **Developments in the Art of Technology**
   Significant leaps in technological achievement have been made possible, in large part, through creative problem solving. It has resulted in the development of paradigm-shifting technologies such as the internet, cellphones, artificial intelligence, and renewable sources of energy.
   These advancements have not only made our day-to-day lives easier, but they have also given rise to totally new business sectors and potential for the economy.
2. **The Expanding Economy**
   The most important factor contributing to economic expansion is innovation. When businesses innovate, they give birth to new customer bases and avenues of revenue. Because of this, jobs are created, which in turn supports economic activity, which in turn fosters wealth and well-being.
3. **Long-term viability**
   In order to effectively handle global concerns such as climate change and a lack of resources, innovation is very necessary. In order to lessen our negative effects on the environment and create a more sustainable future, sustainable developments such as eco-friendly building materials and renewable energy sources are going to be essential.
4. **Major Steps Forward in Health Care**

There have been amazing advancements made in the field of healthcare, which have resulted in an increase in life expectancy, a marked improvement in the quality of treatment provided, and a wider availability of medical services. Numerous lives have been preserved as a direct result of developments in drugs, medical technology, and medical research.

II. The Core Principles of Working Together

1. **Perspectives from Different Fields of Study**
   The act of collaborating brings together people from a variety of experiences and fields of expertise. This method that crosses disciplinary boundaries frequently results in novel perspectives and novel approaches to problems. When specialists from a variety of professions work together, they are better able to approach difficult challenges with a holistic perspective.
2. **Combining of Available Resources**
   The sharing of resources, whether they be financial, intellectual, or technological, is made possible through the process of collaboration.

This can speed up the process of developing and implementing creative ideas, which may be beyond the capacity of a single entity to accomplish alone.
3. Impact on the World
The concept of collaboration is not restricted by physical location. In today's increasingly globalized world, businesses have the opportunity to cooperate with partners all over the world, giving them access to a vast global network of information, expertise, and resources. This is particularly important when considering how to manage global concerns such as pandemics and climate change.
4. Capacity to Grow

The effects of breakthroughs can be multiplied more rapidly through collaborative efforts. An creative concept or solution can reach a wider audience and have a greater impact on the world at large if it is developed in collaboration with other people.

III. The Mutually Beneficial Partnership

1. The Advancement of Science
Collaboration among scientists, institutions, and even governments is typically the driving force behind significant advancements in the scientific community. Collaboration is essential to the success of scientific endeavors, from the locating of the Higgs boson particle to the development of new genomic techniques.
2. Free and Public Domain Software
The creation of software that is freely available to the public is an excellent illustration of how collaboration can spur innovation. Hundreds of thousands of programmers from all over the world work together on various software development projects, such as Linux, Apache, and Android, to create dependable and user-friendly software that runs the digital world.
3. Forming Alliances and Consortia
Consortia and alliances have been formed to foster innovation across many different industries, including aviation, healthcare, and technology, among others. These types of cooperative endeavors frequently result in the formulation of standards, new best practices, and innovative technological solutions.
4. Innovation Based on Public Participation

Crowdsourcing platforms frequently give rise to the development of novel solutions and products. Businesses such as Kickstarter and

Indiegogo make it possible for individuals and new businesses to work together with members of the public to raise money for and launch new products and services.

IV. Influencing the Course of the Future in Various Industries

1. **Modern equipment**
   Innovation and cooperation are essential to the success of the technology industry. Tech behemoths such as Google, Apple, and Microsoft are actively involved in the formation of partnerships and the acquisition of innovative companies. Open source communities make important contributions to the development of cutting-edge software, and research collaborations drive important advances in a variety of fields, including artificial intelligence, quantum computing, and more.
2. **Health care services**
   In the field of medicine, collaboration and innovative thinking have led to profound shifts in how diseases are diagnosed, treated, and managed. Technologies such as telemedicine, genetics, and medical imaging have all contributed to improvements in patient care. Vaccine development has been sped up because to cross-industry collaborations, which is especially important in light of recent global health crises.
3. **Sustainability and the Role of Energy**
   Innovations in renewable energy sources, energy-efficient technologies, and electric vehicles are driving a change toward sustainability in the energy sector. This shift is being facilitated by the sector's transition to electric vehicles. Collaboration efforts, such as international climate agreements and public-private partnerships, are essential to the process of promoting innovation in environmentally friendly practices.
4. **A formal education**
   E-learning platforms, individualized education, and digital resources are examples of recent advancements that have occurred in the education industry. The rapid proliferation of online education as a result of collaboration between educational establishments and technology companies has increased the availability of high-quality educational options for a more diversified range of students.
5. **The economy**

The term "fintech" refers to the new solutions brought to the financial industry by the field of "financial technology." These solutions include digital payments, blockchain, and robo-advisors. The acceleration of financial innovation and the improvement of consumer experiences are both being driven by collaborative efforts between traditional financial institutions and fintech firms.

V. Obstacles and Things to Take Into Account

1. **Ownership of One's Own Ideas**
   It can be difficult to keep track of ownership and rights to intellectual property when working on collaborative projects. A thoughtful legal framework is required in order to overcome the difficulty of striking a balance between the need to safeguard innovations and the desire to encourage open collaboration.
2. **Problems of an Ethical Nature**
   Concerns regarding ethics are raised whenever significant advances are made in fields such as biotechnology and artificial intelligence. It is imperative that collaborative efforts manage these ethical considerations in order to guarantee that inventions will be beneficial to society while maintaining ethical boundaries.
3. **Coordination and dissemination of information**
   Effective coordination and communication are essential components of successful teamwork. The progression of joint initiatives can be slowed down by a number of factors, including misaligned goals, inadequate communication, and competing interests.
4. **Acceptance of everyone**

It is crucial to make sure that the partnership is open to everyone and diverse. In order to encourage creativity that is both more comprehensive and more egalitarian, collaborative activities ought to include the incorporation of a wide variety of perspectives, backgrounds, and experiences.

VI. The Path That Lies Ahead

1. **Newer technological developments**
   Collaboration will be essential to the development of novel approaches in fields of developing technology such as quantum computing, biotechnology, and space exploration. The implementation and development of these technologies will be driven by scientific research as well as partnerships spanning other industries.
2. **Problems on a Global Scale**
   The globe is currently dealing with a number of critical issues, including climate change, pandemics, and food security. When it

comes to developing long-term solutions to these global problems, innovation and collaboration will be absolutely essential.
3. **The Digitization of Everything**
Innovation and collaborative efforts will continue to be the driving forces behind the ongoing digital transformation of companies and societies. The way that we work, study, and engage with technology will all be significantly altered as a result of this.
4. **Medical Care and Health Services**

The advancement of healthcare and medicine will result in more individualized therapies, the discovery of diseases at an earlier stage, and overall improvements in patient care. The integration of artificial intelligence, genomics, and medical research will be driven by collaborative efforts between researchers, healthcare providers, and technology businesses.

Collaboration and innovation are two powerful forces that drive forward movement and work hand in hand to construct the future. They worked together to revolutionize entire sectors, enhance the quality of life, and find solutions to difficult problems on a worldwide scale. It is abundantly evident that innovation and cooperation will continue to be necessary components in the process of constructing a society that is more connected, egalitarian, and sustainable as we negotiate the complexity and opportunities of the future.

This dynamic team has an infinite amount of potential, and the influence they have had is a lasting tribute to the strength of human creativity when combined with collaborative effort. Innovation and collaboration will continue to be the driving forces that move us toward a brighter and more promising future. This is true regardless of whether we are attempting to solve the mysteries of the universe or tackle the most pressing crises on a global scale.

9.4 Final thoughts on the dynamic duo's potential

The powerful combination of creative thought and cooperative effort has the ability to bring about substantial changes in the world we live in. When harnessed and fostered, these two motivating forces form a synergy that enables us to overcome issues, pioneer new frontiers, and improve the quality of life for both individuals and societies. When we think about their potential, we realize that the future will be full with wonderful chances, but it will also come with duties and things to think about, both of which require our whole attention as a group.

1. Encouraging Creativity and Forward Movement

There is no limit to the capacity of new ideas and collaborative efforts to spawn inventiveness and propel forward progress. This powerful pair has been instrumental in some of humanity's most astonishing accomplishments, such as the successful landing of a human being on the moon and the invention of life-saving medical advancements. Their contribution to encouraging innovation and advancement will be vital as we move forward in this endeavor.

1. Providing Opportunities for Visionaries
   Visionaries are given the ability to envision and create things that were previously considered unattainable thanks to innovation. Innovators such as Elon Musk, who have moved us toward a more environmentally friendly future through the development of electric vehicles and space travel, are excellent examples of how innovation can bring ideas into reality.
2. Finding Solutions to Complicated Problems

The ability to innovate and work together is a significant instrument in the fight against difficult global challenges. Climate change, pandemics, and food security are just a few of the challenges that, in order to be properly addressed, call for new solutions and cooperation across international borders.

II. The Evolution Into the Digital Age

Innovation and collaborative effort are the primary propulsion forces behind the ongoing digital transformation of companies and societies. The potential to revolutionize the ways in which we work, communicate, and learn is enormous in a world that is becoming increasingly interconnected.

1. Creating Havoc in the Industry
   Traditional sectors are being upended by innovative start-up companies working in conjunction with established corporations. The financial industry is being disrupted by fintech, the retail industry is being transformed by e-commerce, and the delivery of medical care is being altered by telemedicine.
2. Participation in the Digital Age

It is essential to make concerted efforts for digital inclusion in order to guarantee that the advantages of digital transformation may be reaped by all members of society. The digital divide needs to be closed in order for equitable progress to be made.

III. Considerations of an Ethical Nature

Ethical considerations are becoming increasingly essential as technological advancement and increased collaboration carry us further into the future. It is imperative that we discuss sensitive topics such as privacy, artificial intelligence, and the ethical application of technology. This dynamic duo's potential will be significantly shaped by the various ethical factors that are taken into account.

1. Intelligent machine ethics

    The use of artificial intelligence is a strong technology that has the potential to revolutionize many different industries as well as our everyday lives. However, this does bring up ethical considerations, such as the possibility of prejudice in computer programs, the protection of personal data, and the effect on employment. To successfully manage these problems, ethical AI frameworks will be absolutely necessary.
2. Protecting Personal Information

The massive amount of data that might be produced by digital technology necessitates the establishment of stringent policies and procedures regarding data privacy. It is essential for governments, businesses, and members of civil society to work together in order to safeguard the data and digital rights of individuals.

IV. Confronting Obstacles on a Global Scale

The reaction to the COVID-19 pandemic serves as a prime example of the potential that may be realized through innovation and teamwork in order to address global concerns. In the face of a disaster, the globe has demonstrated its ability to band together and come up with innovative solutions through collaborative efforts in the production of vaccines, medical research, and global health initiatives.

1. Health on a Global Scale

    New developments in medicine, like as the technology behind mRNA vaccines, have the potential to bring about a sea change in how countries respond to public health threats. In order to effectively handle impending public health concerns, it will be essential for pharmaceutical corporations, government agencies, and research institutes to work together.
2. Climate Change Efforts

The fight against climate change requires significant innovation in the fields of renewable energy and environmentally responsible behaviors. The ability of these breakthroughs to bring about a reduction in global emissions will be shaped by international collaboration in the form of agreements such as the Paris Agreement.

V. Cultivating an Innovation-Friendly Organizational Culture

We need to foster a culture of creativity if we are going to be able to fully grasp the promise that innovation and cooperation hold. This culture supports creativity, is willing to embrace risk, and actively promotes collaboration across disciplinary lines.

1. Formal schooling

   The development of an innovative culture is significantly aided by the participation of educational institutions in the process. Future generations will be more equipped to contribute to the development of the world if they are encouraged to think critically, solve problems, and be creative from a young age.

2. Business Ownership and Control

Many breakthroughs are driven by business owners acting on their own initiative. Innovation and economic growth are both fostered through the cultivation of environments that encourage and applaud the pursuit of entrepreneurial opportunities.

VI. Keeping the Spirit of Innovation and Collaboration Alive

It is imperative that we be cautious in handling obstacles and keeping momentum if we are to preserve the potential offered by this dynamic combo. Protecting intellectual property, fostering diversity in the innovation process, and ensuring that ethical considerations continue to be at the forefront of technical breakthroughs are all necessary steps to take to achieve this goal.

1. Ownership of One's Own Ideas

   It is vital to strike a balance between the protection of intellectual property and open collaboration. It is essential to have legal frameworks that foster innovation while simultaneously protecting the rights of creators and inventors.

2. Acceptance of Differences and Participation

   It is essential to have diverse perspectives and include everyone in creative endeavors and collaborative efforts. Ensuring that voices from people with a variety of experiences and perspectives are heard leads to solutions that are more comprehensive and equitable.

3. Ethical Principles and Guidelines

The establishment of ethical frameworks ought to be at the forefront of technical progress. The potential for creativity and collaboration can be protected by promoting ethical practices, openness, and accountability.

The possibilities that could be realized through innovation and collaboration are numerous and extensive. It is abundantly obvious that these two pillars of progress will continue to be the driving forces that move us toward a world that is brighter and more promising as we manage the complexity and opportunities of the future.

The power of human invention combined with the power of cooperation is demonstrated by the transformative influence of this dynamic combination, which is a tribute to the power of human genius. Innovation and collaboration will continue to be the driving forces that empower us to design a future that is defined by progress, inclusion, and sustainability. This is true regardless of whether we are attempting to solve the secrets of the universe or address the most pressing concerns on a global scale. As we move forward, it is our duty to cultivate and cultivate this potential for the betterment of our world so that we can move forward.

Printed in the USA
CPSIA information can be obtained
at www.ICGtesting.com
LVHW012015250124
769291LV00015B/637